Hollywood's Other Women

Also by Alex Barris:

The Pierce Arrow Showroom Is Leaking
Hollywood's Other Men

Hollywood's Other Women

Alex Barris

South Brunswick and New York: A. S. Barnes and Company
London: Thomas Yoseloff Ltd

A. S. Barnes and Co., Inc.
Cranbury, New Jersey 08512

Thomas Yoseloff Ltd
108 New Bond Street
London W1Y OQX, England

Library of Congress Cataloging in Publication Data

Barris, Alex.
   Hollywood's other women.

   Includes index.
   1. Moving-picture actors and actresses. I. Title.
PN1998.A2B364   791.43′028′0922   74-6933
ISBN 0-498-01488-6

PRINTED IN THE UNITED STATES OF AMERICA

To Ted and Katy,
who have met many of these women
on the TV "Late Show"

Contents

Introduction

In movies, if not always in life, everybody's gain is somebody else's loss. A "good guy" couldn't win without a "bad guy" losing; if justice triumphs, then evil must fail, or vice versa—and in movies it's more versa than vice.

So it was with Hollywood heroines. In truth, part of the satisfaction of winning was the knowledge that someone else lost. Audiences could feel contentment in seeing Claudette Colbert in the final clinch with Fred MacMurray; but this contentment was that much more heightened by the awareness that Claudette had to clobber some insufferable society snob in order to win Fred for keeps.

All this may sound terribly obvious and even naive, but it helps to explain the function of the Other Woman in Hollywood movies, from the 1930s on.

It's a matter of speculation as to whether the moviemakers of Hollywood's so-called Golden Era consciously (or even cynically) concocted these fairytale values in order to please the largely female-controlled audience; or whether they themselves had come to believe in such unreality. The latter theory is easily supportable, at least with regard to the more successful movies, if only because a certain amount of sincerity in creating such projects has a way of making the results more convincing.

In any case, the triumph of a heroine was always that much more rewarding if it was gained over formidable odds. Beating out a rival, however synthetic, was usually the easiest route to audience approval.

Often, in fact, the more synthetic the rival appeared to be, the more satisfying was her ultimate defeat by our squeaky-clean heroine. One had to be careful, in planning the romantic dramas or comedies, that the Other Woman was not made too appealing, perhaps for fear of confusing the audience or risking the destruction of the audience's clear identification with the heroine.

The Other Woman, therefore, had to live (on the screen, that is) by as rigid a code as did any pure heroine. The evolution of this code had much to do with the development of a style of playing and a "type" of actress who was acceptable in Other Woman roles, as will be seen in the first chapter of this book.

But just as the making of any successful movie requires the combined talents and crafts of many people, the making of a successful movie heroine required the support of an assortment of Other Women.

Thus far, only one has been mentioned, the Rival. Perhaps the second most important was the Mother—his or hers, it didn't matter which. Maternal protectiveness has always been a useful ingredient of drama, and the Hollywood movies didn't fail to exploit its potential, both in serious films and in comedies or musicals.

Another method of building up the heroine—or maybe helping to interpret her to the audience—was the use of a close friend, uninvolved herself in the romance but on hand to soothe hurt feelings, help unscramble ridiculous misunderstandings that movie plots abound in, or to comment wryly on the bumpiness of the road to love.

9

These are but a few of the categories of Other Women to be examined in subsequent chapters. Each helped to create a market for a certain "type" of actress, each helped lay the boundaries within which a great many actresses over the past four decades have had to exist.

As with male players, some of the actresses were able to glide from one category into another, some serving an apprenticeship as Other Women before moving up to stardom, others maturing and developing so as to be able to slip gracefully from one type of Other Woman into another.

But it is perhaps significant that the majority of the women to be surveyed in this book spent most of their working years in other than leading-lady roles.

In the years encompassed roughly by the four decades of talking pictures, one of the basic myths of the American dream gradually disintegrated. This was the myth that there's always room at the top for anyone with enough talent and determination to get there.

Most of the ladies in this book have had ample reason to recognize the fallacy of this theory. They had (and some still have) both the talent and the determination. Some of them lacked that elusive quality that separates actresses from stars. Others probably never got the opportunity to display their talents effectively. Still others achieved stardom and were eventually driven downward by the ravages of age or the fickleness of public tastes.

All of them were probably grateful, in the long run, that Hollywood movies did require and make use of rivals, mothers, friends, and other such characters that they could play again and again, sometimes carving out careers for themselves that were more secure and more enduring than life at the top could be.

And all of us—assuming that we are movie fans to begin with—should be grateful to them for the stalwart support they have given the leading ladies of American films.

Hollywood's Other Women

1

The Classic Bitch

The sociologists can debate why it should be that the vast American public has for so long harbored a murkily resentful attitude toward that upper stratum of the population known vaguely as "society."

It's perfectly understandable that people with relatively little money should lose no love over those with plenty of it. But the requirements of American popular fiction—and more especially of Hollywood movies—go well beyond that. They decree that the upper crust, the 400, high society, or whatever else they are called, are snobbish, heartless, phony, pretentious creatures who exist on champagne and caviar, spend their days foreclosing mortgages and their evenings dozing off at dull opera performances. The men all went to Harvard or Yale, inherited their money, and are unable to tie their own shoelaces; the women have their faces lifted annually, mistreat their help, and have casual affairs with their chauffeurs or each other's husbands. They are a sorry lot, no less suspect for their ostentatious support of cultural or intellectual pursuits.

This attitude is as old as the country and as new as current events. In the 1930s, Groucho Marx could get howls from movie audiences by insulting that indomitable caricature of the society "dame," Margaret Dumont. In the 1970s Spiro Agnew could make hard hats cheer by attacking effete intellectual snobs. Both on stage (in "sophisticated" New York) and on film, *The Unsinkable Molly Brown* had mass appeal because its heroine was an earthy, irreverent, frankly lowbrow woman who thumbed her nose at the wealthy and powerful.

While it would be foolish to suggest that Hollywood invented this attitude, it would be foolhardy to deny that the movies exploited it successfully, again and again, in countless romantic comedies, musicals, and dramas.

It's important to remember that moviemakers have long believed, with or without justification, that it is the women of America who decide which movie will be supported at the box office; the husband goes along, generation after generation, docile and mute, to Loretta Young Cinderella stories, Irene Dunne comedies, Bette Davis dramas, or Ali McGraw tearjerkers. (It might be argued that films with action and violence also do very well at theaters, but that implies that they do well over the objections of women patrons, who really don't like all that gore—an assumption that isn't notably realistic.)

The point is that in the days when Hollywood stereotypes were being molded, moviemakers saw the wisdom of pitting sympathetic heroines like Colbert or Dunne against eccentrically drawn society snobs—classic bitches. There was double victory in seeing the heroine win her man and simultaneously get the better of some sleek society dame dripping diamonds and venom.

The balance had to be there: if the heroine was wholesome, unaffected, and sincere, the rival had to

13

be perfidious, artificial, and conniving. In a "serious" drama or love story, she had to be convincingly sinister; in a comedy, she could be transparent, outrageously overdrawn. Either way, it worked. Whether the women in the audience hated them deeply or were able to laugh at their ludicrous posing, there was gratification in seeing these classic bitches go down to defeat at the hands of clever Claudette or innocent Irene. It was the heroine, after all, who was the movie fan's surrogate, and if the womanly virtues of sincerity, purity, and loyalty could be seen right up there on the silver screen to triumph over phony culture and ill-gotten riches, all was right with the world and the visit to the Bijou was its own reward.

Not every story, of course, could conveniently offer a society snob as rival to the heroine. But the balance between winner and loser could still be maintained in other ways. If there was no place for society in the story, the Classic Bitch could still be there in different guise. She could be less wealthy or cultured but still representative of the forces of evil. She might be a crook or a wanton woman, a scheming, heartless wife whose gloomy husband turns to our heroine for understanding, a fortune hunter against whom the heroine must protect the beguiled hero, a siren who tempts the imperfect husband of our heroine, or a shrewish wife who feigns illness to keep her long-suffering husband by her side.

It is a tribute to some of the actresses who played Other Women that they could perform many of these variations with virtuoso skill and considerable conviction.

Surely one of the best of them all was Mary Astor, whose film career began back in the silent era, hit some flat valleys and a few memorable peaks, and spanned several decades of movie acting.

Her finely chiseled beauty served her well, but she didn't rely on it alone. There was bite to her acting, particularly when she was in the role of the Other Woman, although she was also effective in sympathetic parts.

In films from the mid 1920s, she was earning top money when talkies came along, her combination of angelic looks and sultry manner winning wide public approval. One of her early talking pictures was *Holiday* (1930), based on Philip Barry's hit play of the time. She and Ann Harding were sisters, daughters of a tycoon. Mary became engaged to Johnny Case (Robert Ames), but the romance foundered when their values clashed: Johnny wanted to have a holiday from work while he was still young enough to enjoy it; Julia (Miss Astor) thought this frivolous and irresponsible. In time, sister Ann Harding turned out to be closer to Johnny's ideal and he switched sisters in mid-romance. Mary Astor was the perfect Classic Bitch—poised, attractive, articulate, assertive, hard as nails.

For the next decade, Mary Astor alternated between sympathetic roles (*Dodsworth, The Prisoner of Zenda*) and Classic Bitches. Somehow, she leaps to mind more vividly in the latter category.

She betrayed Richard Dix in *The Lost Squadron*. She was Lilyan Tashman's rival in *Those We Love*. She was Jean Harlow's unsuccessful rival (for Clark Gable) in *Red Dust*. She was Herbert Marshall's nasty wife in *Woman Against Woman*. She was comically vicious in *Midnight*, with Claudette Colbert and Don Ameche. She was a giddy heiress in *The Palm Beach Story*, with Colbert and Joel McCrea.

Proving that there is occasionally some justice in Hollywood, she won an Academy Award for one of her strongest supporting performances—in *The Great Lie* (1941), starring Bette Davis and George Brent—and of course, she was the most hateful of Classic Bitches.

In *The Great Lie,* she played the ambitious concert pianist who takes Brent away from the mousy (!) Miss Davis. After eloping, they learn their marriage was illegal. By now, Brent has come to his senses and he leaves Mary and returns to Bette, who gladly marries him. With Brent gone conveniently overseas, Mary discovers she is pregnant. But being a Classic Bitch she doesn't want the child, nor the world to know of its existence. Noble Bette takes her to a deserted Arizona ranch, acts as midwife and ends up taking the baby as her own—with Mary's blessing. Only after Brent returns (in true movieland tradition, he had been reported dead) does Mary reappear to threaten Bette's now idyllic life. She proposes to expose Bette's lie, confident that it is only the baby that now ties George to Bette.

When the truth is known, Brent says he still loves Bette and is even willing to give the child back to Mary. In a rare departure from rigid Classic Bitchiness, Mary magnanimously walks out, leaving

The Great Lie. The perfect Classic Bitch pose. Bette Davis, eventual winner, is off to the side as Mary Astor snuggles closer to George Brent. (Warner Brothers, 1941)

both baby and Brent to our Bette.*

Miss Astor is not, however, an actress to be remembered for only one film. If the limit were two, the other one would have to be the picture in which she brought to life that other type of Classic Bitch, not high-born and snobbish but sultry and ruthless.

---

* On at least one occasion, *The Great Lie* was shown on television when the attendant on duty got too wrapped up in his comic book. He got a few reels switched, so that viewers first saw the scene in the Arizona cabin when Bette helped deliver Mary's baby, and THEN the scene in which Mary announced her pregnancy.

It happened also to be one of the best private-eye movies in the history of films, the 1941 version of *The Maltese Falcon,* directed by John Huston.

Here she was Brigid O'Shaughnessy, toying with the affections of Sam Spade, coquettishly proclaiming her badness and luring him into more and more danger in her greedy quest of "the bird." Even in the last moments of this excellent film, when Humphrey Bogart (as Spade) has blown the whistle on her and turned her over to the police, one cannot help but admire the way Miss Astor tries to work her feminine charms in one last des-

The Maltese Falcon. Mary Astor is all charm in this early scene from John Huston's taut melodrama. At left is Lee Patrick, and Humphrey Bogart is the Astorogler. (Warner Brothers, 1941)

perate attempt to escape punishment for her deeds. Had she not already dazzled Academy members with her work in *The Great Lie* the same year, she might well have won an Oscar for *The Maltese Falcon,* and with as much justification.

Inevitably, there was the sequel with Bogart—*Across the Pacific*—but her role was enigmatic, murky, and the film simply didn't come off as well.

By the mid-1940s, age had forced her into a swamp of mother roles. She surfaced periodically, playing aging society bitches and over-the-hill trollops for another decade. Never one to fit comfortably into the Hollywood mold, Miss Astor often

went her own way, spurning long-term contracts, even avoiding "star" status because she didn't want the responsibility. But she has left us many finely etched portraits of Classic Bitches and certainly ranks high among the handful of memorable actresses in that category.

Before leaving Mary Astor, it's perhaps worth mentioning another of her earlier films, if only because this role was something of a switch. It was the 1932 comedy, *The Little Giant,* in which Edward G. Robinson was a reformed gangster trying to buy respectability. Miss Astor was the well-bred, sympathetic, recently impoverished girl from an "old" fam-

16

Act of Violence. Outcast Van Heflin is aided by an over-the-hill Mary Astor in this potboiler, filmed twenty-eight years after her movie debut. (MGM, 1949)

ily, who helps Robinson to avoid some of the pitfalls of his course. The primary pitfall was a chilly society snob, a Classic Bitch in the comic genre who, aided by her equally phony family, tries to separate Robinson from his money. Miss Astor was sweet and understanding, a perfect counterpoint to the actress who was this film's Classic Bitch.

That actress was Helen Vinson, and although she is not now nearly as well remembered as Mary Astor, she played her share of Classic Bitches in the 1930s. Miss Vinson was blond and icy and wore a perpetual smile that gave her the air of a reigning monarch deigning to look down aloofly upon her humble subjects. In *The Little Giant*, with the deliciously corrupt Berton Churchill as her father, she took advantage of Robinson's foolish longing for a place in society and very nearly milked him dry before the good Miss Astor helped Eddie see the light.

Helen Vinson played similar roles in many movies. She was Gary Cooper's possessive wife in *The Wedding Night*, whose title didn't refer to their wed-

ding; she sneered at Claudette Colbert and Charles Boyer in *Private Worlds;* she was a society bitch in *Live, Love, and Learn*, with Robert Montgomery and Rosalind Russell; she was a bitchy wife in *Vogues of 1938* (Warner Baxter and Joan Bennett) and again in *Broadway Bill* (Baxter and Myrna Loy); and the cold other woman in *Married and in Love.* She was Ann Sheridan's rival in *Torrid Zone*, a James Cagney-Pat O'Brien film, and was an amusing society bitch in *Nothing but the Truth*, with Bob Hope and Paulette Goddard.

The 1930s seemed to spawn a whole school of Classic Bitches. Miss Vinson was typical, but she by no means monopolized the field. There were also Lilyan Tashman and Veree Teasdale and Freida Inescourt and Virginia Bruce and Marjorie Gateson and Genevieve Tobin and Hedda Hopper (before she became a gossip columnist) and Doris Nolan, who played the Mary Astor role in the 1938 remake of *Holiday,* with Katharine Hepburn and Cary Grant. Some became (or had been) stars. Others went on and on, losing leading men to more wholesome American heroines, occasionally doing parodies of the Classic Bitch roles they had played so expertly in younger years.

Virginia Bruce, like some other actresses in this category, alternated between playing leading ladies in B pictures and Classic Bitches in more expensive films. Although she had been around since the early talking movies, her career reached a kind of peak in *Born To Dance,* a 1936 musical that starred

The Little Giant. Status-seeking racketeer Edward G. Robinson is already in the clutches of wily Helen Vinson in this comedy. (Warner Brothers, 1933)

Born To Dance. Virginia Bruce looks pretty cozy with James Stewart, but he eventually danced off with Eleanor Powell. (MGM, 1936)

Eleanor Powell and James Stewart. Miss Bruce was that familiar figure, the icy Broadway star who walks out on the show just in time for Eleanor to tap her way to stardom and into Stewart's heart. But as the Classic Bitch, Virginia Bruce had at least one memorable moment: trying to seduce Stewart by singing (in her own quite pleasant voice, incidentally) Cole Porter's "I've Got You Under My Skin."

Miss Bruce lost Franchot Tone to Maureen O'Sullivan in *Between Two Women;* she was the other woman in *Hired Wife,* with Brian Aherne and Rosalind Russell; she was the third party in *Wife, Doctor, and Nurse,* with Warner Baxter and Loretta Young. She also played leading roles opposite Melvyn Douglas, Fredric March, and George Brent, but with less memorable results. Her singing voice was used again in *Let Freedom Ring* (1939), one of Nelson Eddy's few films without Jeanette MacDonald, and one of his least successful.

The brunette counterpart of Virginia Bruce was Gail Patrick, an actress of considerable beauty and icy poise who had her fling at B picture leads before finding that she was more acceptable as the Classic Bitch. She always played characters with names like Cynthia Wentworth or Isobel Grayson, names one almost expected to find in the social register.

One of her best Classic Bitch roles was in the noted comedy *My Man Godfrey,* in which she played Carole Lombard's snooty sister. Like Carole, she had eyes for William Powell, the Godfrey of the title, a down-at-the-heels gentleman whom Carole brings home from a hobo jungle and turns into the family butler. When Godfrey won't give Gail a tumble, she turns her efforts to getting rid of him.

Continuing to pay her dues as a Hollywood Classic Bitch, Miss Patrick turned up in *My Favorite Wife,* playing Cary Grant's second wife. Naturally, the first wife (Irene Dunne) turns up alive and well, as first spouses had a way of doing in movies of the time and Gail is promptly sent packing.

She was the other woman in *Love Crazy,* with William Powell and Myrna Loy; and a snob in *Brewster's Millions,* and *Claudia and David.* Unlike most of her sisters in snobbery, Gail Patrick deserted film acting before it could discard her. She turned to television and became one of the few successful women producers in that medium, most notably as producer of the long-running "Perry Mason" series.

Two lesser known but equally effective Other Women were Katherine Alexander and Barbara O'Neil.

Miss Alexander first made life miserable for Bette Davis and Ian Hunter in *The Girl from Tenth Avenue,* a 1935 epic in which she first jilted Hunter and then tried to win him back from Bette.

She was a scornful in-law in *Splendor,* with Miriam Hopkins and Joel McCrea, and a meddling sister given to fainting spells in *She Married Her Boss,* with Claudette Colbert and Melvyn Douglas.

Miss Alexander tangled with Bette Davis again in 1937 in another Warners film titled *That Certain Woman.* This time she played Ian Hunter's unloving wife, while Bette was his secretary. Bette has a brief marriage with playboy Henry Fonda—just long enough to become pregnant. Boss Hunter, a tower of sympathetic jelly, helps take care of Bette's child, but later, when Hunter dies, Miss Alexander charges that her late husband was the

Between Two Women. Both the title and the photo illustrate Franchot Tone's dilemma, but the way he's facing tips off the ending. (MGM, 1937)

My Man Godfrey. Sisters Gail Patrick and Carole Lombard were both interested in William Powell, but it was Carole who won him. (Universal, 1936)

My Favorite Wife. Cary Grant's favorite spouse was Irene Dunne, but Irene had to fight off Gail Patrick (next to Grant) to get him back. Mary Lou Harrington and Scotty Beckett are the youngsters, Ann Shoemaker the older woman. (RKO, 1940)

Katherine Alexander. Chic and handsome, this actress was kept busy in the 1930s, usually playing a Classic Bitch.

Gone with the Wind. This all-time favorite movie gave Barbara O'Neil a rare chance to play a sympathetic role, as Vivien Leigh's mother. (MGM, 1939)

21

Barbara O'Neil. Coldly attractive, Miss O'Neil made a
full-time living losing men to bigger stars in the
1930s and 1940s.

father of Bette's child. In the end, Fonda returns (handily shedding a second wife) and he, Bette, and the child are reunited.

The role of unloved spouse was similar to one of Barbara O'Neil's most successful Classic Bitch parts. This was in another Bette Davis film, *All This and Heaven, Too.* Miss O'Neil was the invalid wife of Charles Boyer and Bette was hired as governess to their children. The suspicious wife becomes convinced that her husband is carrying on with the help and orders Bette fired. This is followed by the death of the wife, the suicide of the husband, and much sympathy for the long-suffering and clearly innocent Bette.

Barbara O'Neil had much the same sort of assignment in *When Tomorrow Comes,* an attempted sequel to the very successful *Love Affair,* with Charles Boyer and Irene Dunne. In this tearjerker, she was Boyer's demented wife and Miss Dunne the lady he loves.

As if being typed as Other Woman wasn't bad enough, Miss O'Neil had the bad luck to become typed as a deranged woman, a role she was assigned yet again in *Shining Victory,* with James Stephenson and Geraldine Fitzgerald.

Once, at least, she managed to get a different sort of role in a first-rate film: she was Scarlet O'Hara's mother in *Gone with the Wind,* and although she was generally overlooked in this festival of virtuoso performances, she was effective as the mistress of Tara. But even here she had to have a mental breakdown before the end of the picture. ("We'll get Barbara O'Neil for Scarlet's mother," one can almost hear David Selznick commanding. "She's great at losing her marbles.")

Better known Classic Bitches were Miriam Hopkins and Kay Francis, coupled here only because their careers offer some similarities. Both were fairly big names, both just missed becoming top-drawer stars.

In fairness, Kay Francis came closer to genuine stardom in the early 1930s, but her appeal faded well before her ambition. Long before William Powell and Myrna Loy became a popular screen team, Powell and Miss Francis had worked together in several films, among them the highly successful tearjerker, *One Way Passage.*

But she had a haughty way about her and playing Other Women seems to have been an inevitability. She was the faithless wife of a banker in

The Feminine Touch. Rosalind Russell, here looking like the interloper, was really the heroine of this comedy, Kay Francis the Other Woman. That's Don Ameche at left. (MGM, 1941)

Wonder Bar (with Al Jolson, in 1934) and the loser in a Lubitsch triangle comedy, *Trouble in Paradise.* She was a catty, grasping wife in a 1939 film, *In Name Only,* with Carole Lombard and Cary Grant. She was the other woman in *The Feminine Touch,* with Rosalind Russell and Don Ameche. And she was Walter Huston's two-timing wife in *Always in My Heart.*

Miriam Hopkins was a stage actress before Hollywood beckoned, only to find she didn't fit easily into some of the roles planned for her. Her career went up and down in the early 1930's, but she turned out to have a strong enough personality that Other Woman roles suited her best.

In 1936, Samuel Goldwyn filmed a mutilated version of Lillian Hellman's play, *The Children's Hour.* The sensitive censors forced drastic changes, but what emerged was still an effective triangle drama, with Joel McCrea and Merle Oberon as the leads and Miriam Hopkins most impressive as the extra girl. The film was titled *These Three.*

She had an even meatier role in *The Old Maid,* with Bette Davis as the star. This one was almost a turnaround of *The Great Lie,* which it actually preceded. It was Bette who had the illegitimate baby this time—sired by George Brent, who had been jilted by Miriam, Bette's cousin—and Miriam who took in Bette and her infant. The baby grew up to become Jane Bryan, who regarded Hopkins as her

Always in My Heart. Kay Francis was a less-than-ideal wife to Walter Huston in this romantic drama. (Warner Brothers, 1942)

mother and Bette as her spinster aunt. Bette allowed Miriam to legally adopt young Jane and even chickened out on her threat to reveal the truth on the eve of Jane's wedding. Miss Hopkins's unyielding strength provided a fine contrast to Bette's emotional turmoil.

Davis and Hopkins tangled once more in the 1943 film, *Old Acquaintance.* This time around, they were both writers, Miriam becoming famous as an author of trashy novels, Bette devoted to more scholarly efforts. Their feuding starts when Miriam's husband (John Loder) leaves her, intending to marry Bette, who rejects him. It goes on for a couple of decades, ending only after (are you ready for this?) Bette valiantly abandons her plan to marry Gig Young, who is in love with Miriam's daughter.

Miss Hopkins's flair for conveying relentless bitchiness robbed her of many more sympathetic roles and kept her stuck in strong Other Woman roles for some years. She was Brian Donlevy's pitiless wife in *A gentleman After Dark* (1942) and a society bitch in *The Mating Season,* a 1951 comedy.

In time she was reduced to playing aunts: Olivia de Havilland's in *The Heiress,* and Shirley Mac-Laine's in *The Children's Hour,* a remake in which Miss MacLaine played the part first played by Hopkins when it was dry-cleaned into *These Three.* But she had one more good bitchy wife role left in her: this was as Laurence Olivier's nagging spouse in *Carrie,* with Jennifer Jones as Olivier's leading lady.

Rosalind Russell, whose long career was to lead

The Old Maid. Off to the side again is Bette Davis, as George Brent warms to Miriam Hopkins. But Bette bore his child. (Warner Brothers, 1939)

Carrie. Laurence Olivier sits through a tongue-lashing from Miriam Hopkins, who soon lost him to Jennifer Jones. (Paramount, 1952)

Manproof. Rosalind Russell calls on Myrna Loy. The subject of their clash was Franchot Tone, and Loy won him. (MGM, 1938)

The Women. Rosalind Russell looks innocent of any wrongdoing in this scene with Norma Shearer, center, and Phyllis Povah. But she was the gossip who caused much of the trouble in this comedy. (MGM, 1939)

up and down the ladder to box-office success, paid her dues in Other Woman roles in the 1930s. She insinuated herself briefly between William Powell and Myrna Loy in *Evelyn Prentice* (1934) and between Clark Gable and Jean Harlow, the following year, in *China Seas,* playing a society girl whose appeal was a sharp contrast to Harlow's. In *Manproof* (1938) she was the other woman who lost Franchot Tone to Myrna Loy.

In 1936, Miss Russell starred in an unusual drama called *Craig's Wife,* in which she managed to lose her husband (John Boles) even though there was really no other woman. George Kelly's Pulitzer Prize-winning play presented a strong-willed, domineering woman who ran her house with meticulous care and tried to run her husband's life the same way. The husband eventually realizes that Harriet Craig loves only her spotless house and walks out, leaving her to enjoy it alone. Although the picture was not a great success, Rosalind Russell got good reviews and, perhaps inadvertently, set a pattern for herself that would become hard to escape: she was a convincing bitch.

Three years later, however, it paid off handsomely when she got the plum role of Sylvia in Claire Boothe's *The Women.* This crisp, witty film, directed by George Cukor, had an all-female cast that included Norma Shearer, Joan Crawford, Mary Boland, Paulette Goddard, and Joan Fontaine. Crawford was the vamp who tried to steal Shearer's (unseen) husband. But it was Rosalind Russell, as the catty gossip, Sylvia, who had some of Miss Boothe's most biting lines and delivered them with great style. She was the Classic Bitch of the 1930s.

One cannot leave that decade without some mention of two more Classic Bitches, both of whom spoofed the category, albeit in different ways: Binnie Barnes and Margaret Dumont.

Miss Barnes, a statuesque beauty of Grecian marble, had her own special way of playing beguiling bitches without ever losing that shade of underplayed humor that made her appeal so special. She used an artificial smile that barely covered an "oh-my-girdle-is-killing-me" expression and romped her way through a score of bitchy roles.

As early as 1933, in the memorable Charles Laughton film, *The Private Life of Henry VIII,* she was indulging in that time-honored tradition of Other Women, scene-stealing. She made a beautiful Catherine Howard, dazzling Henry with her charms and

The Private Life of Henry VIII. Binnie Barnes was delightfully bitchy in this famous film starring Charles Laughton. (United Artists, 1933)

winning his notoriously fickle heart. Her best moment came in a scene in which the king goes stealthily to visit Catherine in her apartment. When he raps lightly on her door, she asks who is there.

"Henry," says the king.

"Henry who?" asks Miss Barnes.

Thus auspiciously launched on a career of screen bitchery, Binnie went on to play a spy in *Rendezvous,* with William Powell and Rosalind Russell; an aloof Lillian Russell to Edward Arnold's *Diamond Jim;* an enigmatic countess in *Sutter's Gold;* Robert Taylor's bitchy fiancée in *Small Town Girl,* with Janet Gaynor in the title role; a snobbish wife in *Skylark;* a society bitch in the remake of *Holiday,* with Grant and Hepburn.

Miss Barnes went on through the 1940s: with Nelson Eddy and Jeanette MacDonald in *I Married an Angel;* with Walter Pidgeon and Deborah Kerr in *If Winter Comes,* with Franchot Tone and Veronica Lake in *The Hour Before Dawn.* Even when the pictures were less than splendid, Binnie Barnes's presence often gave them a lift.

In time, she married a Hollywood executive (Mike Frankovich) and was absent from the screen for more than a decade. Then, in 1972, she turned up in a fine role, but one that properly belongs in another chapter.

The redoubtable Margaret Dumont, already a favorite with cultists, was almost in a class by herself. If Binnie Barnes quietly poked fun at the society

Sutter's Gold. The mysterious countess, Binnie Barnes, joins Robert Warwick for a little drink. (Universal, 1936)

she was portraying, Margaret Dumont hit it with a shovel—and always deadpan.

In seven Marx Brothers pictures, she was as necessary a part of their act as Groucho's cigar, Chico's Italian accent, or Harpo's honker. She personified stuffy society, a splendidly regal woman, virtually attached to a lorgnette and given to uttering, with outraged dignity, such feeble rejoinders as "Really!"

She was a prop, to be knocked down, to get pies in the face, to suffer insolence and insult, to be ridiculed and deflated. She was the symbol of the monied class and the more she was cut down by the irreverent Marx Brothers the more audiences howled.

There were ground rules, which she never broke: she must never let down her guard, never indicate in any way that it was all in fun. She had to be as straight-faced as Ned Sparks, yet never get a laugh on her own. She had to be the butt of every joke and bear it without grinning.

From *Cocoanuts,* in 1929, through *The Big Store,* in 1941, she served Groucho, Chico, and Harpo loyally. She was almost a Marx Sister. Even though she later lent her magnificent presence to such other comics as Jack Benny (*The Horn Blows at Midnight*) and Danny Kaye (*Up in Arms*), she will always be inextricably associated with the brothers Marx.

Somehow, the Classic Bitch seems to have gone into a decline beginning somewhere in the 1940s. Perhaps America's resentment against the upper class-

Cocoanuts. The inimitable Margaret Dumont listens skeptically to the irrepressible Groucho Marx. (Paramount, 1929)

Ninotchka. Ina Claire uses all her wiles to keep Melvyn Douglas away from Greta Garbo in this delicious Ernst Lubitsch comedy. (MGM, 1939)

Congo Maisie. Rita Johnson, center, played the wife of ailing Shepperd Strudwick in this one. That's John Carroll at left, and Ann Sothern as Maisie. It was one of Miss Johnson's less bitchy roles. (MGM, 1940)

A Woman's Face. That's Osa Massen turning it on for Melvyn Douglas, but he eventually saw through her, and straight to Joan Crawford. (MGM, 1941)

Invitation. Ruth Roman, foreground, did her damndest to get rid of Dorothy McGuire, but in the end Dorothy won Van Johnson. (MGM, 1952)

The Sound of Music. If Eleanor Parker looks distraught in this scene with Christopher Plummer, it may be because she knows she doesn't stand a chance against Julie Andrews, all those darling kids, and a Rodgers and Hammerstein score. (20th Century-Fox, 1965)

Executive Suite. William Holden comforts Nina Foch.
Actually, she was just trying to win his sympathy, etc.
(MGM, 1954)

Bright Leaf. Gary Cooper and Patricia Neal as bride and groom, with friend Jack Carson looking on. In time, Gary was turned off by her selfishness. (Warner Brothers, 1950)

es was sated during the depression years. Perhaps the stock character became too much a caricature and was no longer acceptable in any but the broadest comedies—of which there have been notably fewer.

Whatever the reasons, the 1950s and 1960s offer far fewer examples of actresses who made careers of playing Classic Bitches. Some, however, come to mind and deserve inclusion here, if only briefly:

Ina Claire in *Ninotchka* (1939), trying every trick in the book to win Melvyn Douglas back from Greta Garbo.

Osa Massen as Melvyn Douglas's sluttish wife in *A Woman's Face,* in 1941.

Rita Johnson in *The Major and the Minor,* with Ginger Rogers and Ray Milland (1942) and in *Susan Slept Here,* with Dick Powell and Debbie Reynolds (1954).

Ruth Roman in *Invitation,* with Van Johnson and Dorothy McGuire (1952), cold and bitchy as Johnson's ex-fiancée.

Nina Foch in *An American in Paris,* with Gene Kelly and Leslie Caron (1951).

Eleanor Parker as Frank Sinatra's nagging wife in *The Man with the Golden Arm* (1955) and as the bitchy baroness in *The Sound of Music* (1965).

Patricia Neal as a selfish Southern Belle in *Bright Leaf,* with Gary Cooper and Lauren Bacall (1950), and as a rich bitch in *Breakfast at Tiffany's* (1961).

Ilka Chase as a Hedda Hopper-type columnist in *The Big Knife* (1955).

Angela Lansbury as a shrew of a wife (to Glenn Ford) in *Dear Heart* (1965), as an ambitious woman in *State of the Union* (1948), and as Kay Kendall's competition in *The Reluctant Debutante* (1958).

Dorothy Malone as a spoiled rich girl in *Written on the Wind* (1957).

Plus Dina Merrill and Carolyn Jones, Ruth Hussey and Dana Wynter, Audrey Totter and Ilona Massey, Patricia Morrison, Gene Tierney, Freida Inescort and Veree Teasdale.

And then there was Alexis Smith. This frosty Canadian beauty first surfaced in Hollywood in 1941 in a minor wartime action film called *Dive Bomber.* The stars were Errol Flynn and Fred MacMurray, feuding and scrapping for all the world as if they were Cagney and O'Brien. Miss Smith had the leading female role, but it was insignificant. She kept turning up every few reels, at a Navy dance or a cocktail party, in a vain effort to tempt Flynn away from his duties. But war was war and Alexis was pushed gently into the background as Flynn and MacMurray took care of more serious business. One can scarcely remember—nor did it matter—whether she ever turned up for the final clinch.

She was equally decorative, and just as unimportant, the following year in *Gentleman Jim,* also with Errol Flynn. In 1943 she got her first Other

The Big Knife. Ilka Chase, center, was a bitchy columnist in this Hollywood story. She tried to sniff out a split between Ida Lupino and Jack Palance. The man in the center background is Paul Langton. (United Artists, 1955)

State of the Union. Angela Lansbury and Katharine Hepburn at odds over Spencer Tracy's political (and personal) future. (MGM, 1948)

Woman role, in a soapy version of *The Constant Nymph,* with Charles Boyer and Joan Fontaine.

Next came a wartime comedy, *The Doughgirls* (1944), which was regarded as witty at the time but seems dreary now. She was one of three newly married girls (Ann Sheridan and Jane Wyman were the others) scrambling for a hotel suite in wartime Washington.

In 1945, she had a thankless Other Woman role in *Rhapsody in Blue,* a highly fanciful biography of George Gershwin, with Robert Alda as the composer and Joan Leslie as the Nice Girl. And in 1946 she turned up in an inferior remake of the Somerset Maugham work, *Of Human Bondage,* this time with Eleanor Parker as the trollop and Paul Henreid as the smitten medical student.

Alexis really came into her own as a Classic Bitch that same year in a comedy-drama titled *One More Tomorrow.* Dennis Morgan and Ann Sheridan were the romantic leads, with Jack Carson aboard as Morgan's lowbrow pal, and Alexis as the society iceberg who can hardly wait to get her hands on playboy Morgan's money.

In one of those stilted society party scenes, Alexis coolly tells John Loder: "I happen to like money. I like the power it brings."

"You are the most selfish woman I've ever met," says Loder.

"Thanks for the compliment, "Alexis replies. "Now get me a drink."

This was Hollywood Classic Bitchery at its best and Alexis went right on with it for the rest of

The Reluctant Debutante. Rex Harrison is about to leave with Angela Lansbury, but Kay Kendall has a parting shot. And she got him, too. (MGM, 1958)

Pride and Prejudice. Freida Inescourt was an old hand at playing Classic Bitches by this time. Here she's with Laurence Olivier, who co-starred with Greer Garson. (MGM, 1940)

I Take This Woman. Veree Teasdale, right, was the loser when Spencer Tracy decided in favor of Hedy Lamarr, left. (MGM, 1940)

Rhapsody in Blue. Despite this loving pose, Robert Alda had more important things on his mind than Alexis Smith. He was playing George Gershwin, and when he got around to girls he picked Joan Leslie. (Warner Brothers, 1945)

One More Tomorrow. Alexis Smith landed Dennis Morgan in this drama, but she later lost out to Ann Sheridan. (Warner Brothers, 1945)

the film. After working girl Sheridan rejects Morgan, he turns to available Alexis—on the rebound, as they used to say—and she promptly jockeys him into marriage. The only shadow to cross Morgan's path is her refusal to have children. Classic Bitches never want children.

But Alexis eventually makes the fatal mistake: she tries to get rid of Morgan's buddy-butler. Any movie fan of the 1940s knows that splitting up Dennis Morgan and Jack Carson was about as likely to succeed as separating Siamese twins. In the end, not even Alexis's most diaphanous negligee can keep Dennis from coming to his senses, marrying the long-suffering Ann Sheridan and hoisting a few with Jack Carson.

In 1947, Miss Smith played a pointless Other Woman role in *The Two Mrs. Carrolls,* a turgid melodrama with Humphrey Bogart and Barbara Stanwyck. Alexis was neither of the Mrs. Carrolls, but she was ear-marked to become the Third, as soon as

Bogey disposed of Number Two (Miss Stanwyck), as he had done Number One. But with two such strong stars and a rather hokey plot, Alexis had little to do but stand around and look tempting, which is really what she did best.

The previous year, Alexis Smith had been cast in a "leading" role in *Night and Day,* another of those Warner Brothers musical biographies. This time the barely recognizable subject was Cole Porter (played by Cary Grant), and Alexis was reduced to standing around in the wings, waiting for him to finish up a clever lyric. In just five years, she had come full circle—back to where she started in *Dive Bomber.*

As so often happened with Hollywood's Other Women, she was dumped into a succession of B pictures, opposite the likes of Ronald Reagan, Robert Douglas, Joel McCrea, and Zachary Scott.

She surfaced briefly (1951) in *Here Comes the Groom,* doing justice to a good comedy role with Bing Crosby and Jane Wyman as the leads. And, as it must to all statuesque Other Women, there came a role in a Bob Hope movie, *Beau James* (1957), in which he impersonated New York's colorful mayor, Jimmy Walker.

In 1959, Alexis still had one good Classic Bitch role left in her. This was in *The Young Philadelphians,* which starred Paul Newman, who dallied with her before settling for the more wholesome Barbara Rush.

That ended, for the next decade, the film career of Alexis Smith, one of the most beautiful of all the Classic Bitches. But then, suddenly it seemed, there was a happy Hollywood-type ending in store for Miss Smith.

The nostalgia craze of the early 1970s, heralded by *No, No, Nanette,* with Ruby Keeler and Patsy Kelly, lasted long enough for Broadway producer-director Harold Prince to put together a musical extravaganza called *Follies.* Starring in this smash hit was that same Alexis Smith, and at the season's end she won a Tony Award for the year.

Not many of Hollywood's Classic Bitches could claim such fortuitous comebacks. But perhaps the belated recognition of Alexis Smith's rather special appeal can stand as an award to those valiant ladies who spent so many years, collectively, at least, losing leading men and laurels to more popular female stars.

South of St. Louis. A secret Confederate spy was the role of Alexis Smith in this oater. The unhappy looking gent is Alan Hale. (Warner Brothers, 1949)

2

Mothers and Other Estrangers

When the famous Radio City Music Hall in New York's Rockefeller Center first opened its doors, in December 1932, it was actually part of a two-theater complex. The other theater was originally called the RKO Roxy, but later changed its name to the Center Theater. This was because even though S. L. (Roxy) Rothafel was managing the new showplace, the older Roxy Theater, now out of his control, sued to prevent use of the Roxy name in connection with the Rockefeller Center movie houses.

Roxy was soon eased out of the new complex as well, and although the Music Hall became a world-famous showplace, the Center Theater, the smaller of the two, became the forgotten relative. In later years it offered ice shows and the like, but for a time it presented new films and stage attractions, though on a smaller scale than the Music Hall's.

In the spring of 1933, the feature film attraction at the Center Theater was called *The Silver Cord,* and it starred Irene Dunne and Joel McCrea, with Frances Dee and Eric Linden as the second leads. McCrea and Linden were brothers, both married, and both marriages were in jeopardy.

The danger was represented by Laura Hope Crews, the possessive, overprotective mother of the two men. In the end, McCrea was strong enough to take his wife away, but Linden, the younger and weaker brother, knuckled under to Mama, much to the chagrin of the tremulous Miss Dee.

For at least one young moviegoer of ten, on his first excursion to one of the "big" theaters, the shocking thing about that film was the realization that anybody's mother could be so cruel or selfish. Perhaps that was why it stayed in his mind for so many years.

But Miss Crews, already in her fifties then, was an old hand at playing such roles. She went on for another decade, alternating between grasping mothers and twittery town gossips. She was Aunt Pitty-Pat in *Gone with the Wind,* gasping with horror at the scandalous goings on about her, a scented lace hanky ever at the ready to cover a sneeze or hide an involuntary giggle. And she snorted and puffed with outrage every time Fredric March aired his unorthodox thoughts (for a clergyman) in *One Foot in Heaven* (1941).

Miss Crews is by no means the most famous mother in movie history, but she naturally occupies a special place in the heart of one who discovered her at an early and impressionable age.

Movie motherhood is far from being the last refuge of aging actresses. Many fine actresses have worked hard to etch indelible portraits of diverse mothers on our consciousness, often providing stories with their basic motivation, frequently making a deeper impression on us than the glamorous and sympathetic stars of the films.

Movie mothers come in assorted sizes and types, and not all of them have been monsters, although

The Silver Cord. Laura Hope Crews is the focal point of this scene, as she was of the movie. Flanking her, from left, are Eric Linden, Frances Dee, Irene Dunne, and Joel McCrea. (RKO, 1933)

Seven Days Leave. Beryl Mercer wasn't Gary Cooper's real mother in this First World Wartime drama, but they adopted each other. (Paramount, 1930)

those are the ones we tend to remember best. They range from rotund and loving (Jane Darwell) to birdlike and sinister (Beaulah Bondi); from regal and forbidding (Gladys Cooper) to scatterbrained and lovable (Spring Byington); from ambitious and hard (Agnes Moorehead) to defeated and pathetic (Jo Van Fleet).

A score of them, and more, are worth recalling and saluting. Once again, it shouldn't be necessary to point out that in singing the praises of these or others of Hollywood's Other Women, no slight is intended to the writers who created the roles or the directors who oversaw their realization. Nevertheless, it is the actresses we remember because they were the ones whose brand of magic looms large on the screen, whose impact we felt, whose individual personalities haunt our memories.

And in the case of actresses playing mothers, the opportunities for gripping our attention were somehow greater; many of the roles themselves allowed for greater display of emotion by the actresses. And what emotions were paraded before us! Such a clutching of breast, such ready tears and breaking voices, such fainting spells and heart attacks, such ready joy at their offsprings' successes, and such deeply felt (and displayed) sadness at their failures. The joys of motherhood are as nothing compared to the joys of portraying them on the screen.

To begin with, there were those darling, dumpy women of the early 1930s who played the mothers

The Little Giant. **Even in an Abbott and Costello slapstick comedy, Mary Gordon provided a touch of warmth. On the right, Elena Verdugo. (Universal, 1946)**

Kidnapped. **Mary Gordon, a popular screen mother of the 1930s, comforts Arlene Whelan in this scene from the Freddie Bartholomew movie. (20th Century-Fox, 1938)**

of scrapping brothers, Irish cops, and slum-bred hoodlums. One remembers Beryl Mercer in the 1931 shocker, *The Public Enemy.* Moviegoers of the day were too entranced to wonder why a nice little Cockney lady should have one son (James Cagney) who sounded like Hell's Kitchen and another (Donald Cook) who talked like a Midwesterner. But she was a dear woman who loved both her boys, so affectionate that she could close her eyes to what Cagney had become, so vulnerable that the film didn't dare show her reaction to his gory demise at the hands of his underworld enemies.

A year before, Miss Mercer had been equally impressive in *Seven Days Leave,* with Gary Cooper. She wasn't Cooper's real mother in this World War One drama, but she adopted him and even helped straighten him out when he toyed with the thought of deserting the army. When he was killed, his medals for bravery were sent to the proud Miss Mercer.

And there was Mary Gordon, as Irish as corned beef and cabbage, stepping in firmly with chin jutting out, to stifle the brawls between her two sons, Pat O'Brien and James Cagney, in *The Irish in Us* (1935) and other such pastiches.

Different from these two mainly in that her speech style was more homegrown was Emma Dunn, who, among other things, was the mother of young Dr. Kildare (Lew Ayres) in several of the movies in that popular series.

41

Dr. Kildare's Crisis. In this, as in several others of the Kildare series, Emma Dunn played Lew Ayres's lovable mom. (MGM, 1940)

Another memorable actress, Sara Allgood, went to Hollywood from Dublin's Abbey Theater and gave a number of impressive performances, often as a superficially grumpy housekeeper with a soft heart. But she also contributed at least one portrait of a mother that rates listing here: as the hard-working Welsh mother of a mining family in *How Green Was My Valley,* which starred Walter Pidgeon, Maureen O'Hara, Donald Crisp, and Roddy McDowall.

Marjorie Main, an actress too readily identified only with the Ma and Pa Kettle series, contributed at least one fine mother performance as Humphrey Bogart's mom in *Dead End* (1937). Hollow-cheeked, wheezy, utterly defeated by her slum prison, she nevertheless has enough moral fiber left to lash out at her gangster son when he returns for a visit and to denounce him as a hoodlum and killer.

One of the busiest and most irresistible mothers of the 1930s was Spring Byington. She first appeared in films in *Little Women* (1933) as Marmee, trying to keep a rein on such lively lasses as Katharine Hepburn, Joan Bennett, Frances Dee, and Jean Parker.

Two years later, she was the mother in *Ah, Wilderness,* a somewhat watered-down version of the Eugene O'Neill play. Her youngest son in the film was Mickey Rooney. In 1937 she played Rooney's mother again in a (then) little-heralded picture that was destined to start an epidemic.

This was *A Family Affair,* the first of the Hardy family series. Despite its huge success, Miss Byington

42

How Green Was My Valley. Donald Crisp and Sara
Allgood were both excellent as the heads of a mining
family in this drama. (20th Century-Fox, 1941)

Marjorie Main. Best remembered for the comedy series *Ma and Pa Kettle,* she nevertheless played some good dramatic roles, sometimes as a mother. This role was in *Shepherd of the Hills.* (Paramount, 1941)

which, in only four years, managed to cram in some seventeen little B pictures before fizzling out.

By 1939, when the Jones Family was retired, Spring Byington was ready (and available) for one of her happiest roles. This was as Mrs. Sycamore, the mother of that mad and lovable family invented by George Kaufman and Moss Hart in *You Can't Take It with You.* They included a grandfather who didn't believe in paying taxes (Lionel Barrymore), one daughter (Ann Miller) who traipsed about in ballet slippers and a tutu, a son-in-law (Dub Taylor) who played the xylophone, a husband (Samuel S. Hinds) who experimented with explosives in his basement, and another daughter (Jean Arthur) who had the temerity to fall in love with a millionaire's son (James Stewart). The lady of this slap-happy household, Miss Byington, fancied herself a painter. The film, joyously directed by Frank Capra, was a smash hit and earned an Oscar for him and an Oscar nomination for Spring Byington.

On through the 1940s and into the 1950s, Miss Byington continued to play nice, slightly daffy mother roles, occasionally branching off to play nice, slightly daffy maiden aunts or heroines' friends. One of her best of these was in a 1941 comedy titled *The Devil and Miss Jones.* She was Jean Arthur's friend, a sweet spinster who worked alongside Jean in a department store. The comic romance between Miss Arthur and Robert Cummings was almost overshad-

was replaced in the next film in that series by Fay Holden, who went on as Mother Hardy for a total of fifteen films, starting in 1938 and limping to a halt ten years later. (But ten years after that, in 1958, there was a woeful attempt to revive the series in *Andy Hardy Comes Home.* By then, Rooney was 36.)

While Fay Holden did hardly anything but Hardy family movies for a decade, Miss Byington had a more fruitful and varied career. The probable reason she was dropped as Mother Hardy was that she had already appeared in what was to become an equally long-lived, if more modestly successful, series of pictures.

In 1936, Fox made a film called *Every Saturday Night,* with Jed Prouty and Spring Byington as the parents of a light-hearted, adventurous, "typically" American family. They were called the Evers, but when the picture won public acceptance it was decided to make a sequel—and change the family name to Jones. Thus was born the Jones Family series

Ah, Wilderness. Spring Byington, second from right, was an irresistible mother. With her here are Aline MacMahon, Mickey Rooney, and Bonita Granville. (MGM, 1935)

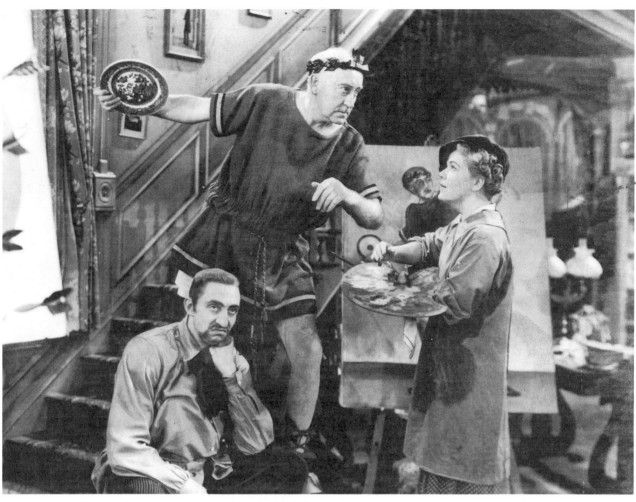

You Can't Take It with You. As Mrs. Sycamore, Spring Byington paints Halliwell Hobbes. The dejected type seated is Mischa Auer. (Columbia, 1938)

Andy Hardy's Blonde Trouble. Ma and Judge Hardy, or Fay Holden and Lewis Stone, who were in all but the first of this series. (MGM, 1944)

Paddy O'Day. That was Jane Withers, the B-picture Shirley Temple. The bundle of warmth to the right is Jane Darwell, one of Hollywood's most beloved mothers. (20th Century-Fox, 1935)

owed by the even more amusing romance between Miss Byington and Charles Coburn.

Although she was in a film as recently as 1960 (*Please Don't Eat the Daisies*) she took several years off in the 1950s to star in her own television series, "December Bride," in which, as one TV critic put it, "Spring hopes eternal."

Perhaps the second most lovable movie mother with any staying power was Jane Darwell. Linguists may argue, but it is this movie buff's distinct impression that Miss Darwell concocted that peculiarly American phrase, "Land sakes." At any rate, nobody else could utter it with more conviction, considering what an inane mouthful it is.

The corpulent Miss Darwell spent some years harrumphing around as a grouchy aunt or a town gossip, tsk-tsking and clucking her disapproval at all

manner of carrying on, sometimes even playing a decidedly unpleasant creature. She was in five Shirley Temple movies in the mid-1930s, never as the moppet's mother, more often than not putting a damper on Shirley's fun.

In 1939 she became a notable movie mother, to a no less notorious character than Jesse James. In the film of that title, she was the down-to-earth Mom of Tyrone (Jesse) Power and Henry (Frank) Fonda, and according to this 20th Century-Fox gospel, it was the mistreating of Mom by some unsavory railroad types that launched the James boys on a life of crime.

The following year brought Miss Darwell her best-known role in one of the finest of all American films, John Ford's honest transfer to the screen of the John Steinbeck novel, *The Grapes of Wrath.* She

46

The Grapes of Wrath. Perhaps the most memorable mother role in American films was played by Jane Darwell, here with Henry Fonda and Russell Simpson. (20th Century-Fox, 1940)

was an unforgettable Ma Joad, a veritable rock of Gibraltar as the de facto head of this crumbling, confused, poverty-stricken family of Okies. Few best supporting actress Academy Awards were as richly deserved as hers for that striking performance.

But Miss Darwell was not one to rest on her well-padded laurels. She had more good supporting roles in *Brigham Young* and *Chad Hanna* (both in 1940), in *The Oxbow Incident* (1943) and *My Darling Clementine* (1946). All these, like most of her films, were for 20th Century-Fox. But in 1941, she turned up in a good mother role in an RKO movie.

It was *All That Money Can Buy,* based on Stephen Vincent Benet's story, "The Devil And Daniel Webster." She was the mother of James Craig, who makes a deal with the devil (slyly played by Walter Huston) and is later saved by the cleverness of Edward Arnold, as Webster.

Jane Darwell continued acting through the 1950s, although in lesser roles for the most part. At the age of 84, she appeared briefly but charmingly as a flower vendor in *Mary Poppins.* She died three years later.

Also active in the 1930s, although perhaps less well remembered by now, were a trio of scatter-brained movie mothers who belong properly with Spring Byington. They were Mary Boland, Alice Brady, and Billie Burke.

Miss Boland, an appealing comedienne somewhat more animated than Margaret Dumont but equally outrageous in her buffoon interpretation of fraudulent society, is probably best remembered for her many screen comedies with Charles Ruggles. They were almost the Maggie and Jiggs of the movies, she forever trying to climb socially, he being earthy and guileless.

They worked together in such films as *If I Had a Million, Six of a Kind, Early to Bed, People Will Talk,* and most importantly in *Ruggles of Red Gap,* in which the pretentious Miss Boland, nouveau riche down to her flashy diamonds, has to be taught manners by Charles Laughton, the English butler.

Miss Boland played a giddy, impractical mother in a number of her films. Most of the time she was preoccupied with putting on airs in hopes of landing a rich husband for some daughter or other. Perhaps the best of these roles was in *Pride and Prejudice,* which starred Greer Garson and Laurence Olivier.

Alice Brady's career started on the stage and then led her to silent films. She specialized in fluttery matrons and was effective in such films as *The Gay*

Brigham Young. Jane Darwell protected youngsters from all manner of danger. With her in this scene are Dickie Jones and Ann Todd. (20th Century-Fox, 1940)

Pride and Prejudice. A fainting spell often helped keep the young ones in line. Mary Boland, flanked by Maureen O'Sullivan and Greer Garson. Looking on is Edmund Gwenn. (MGM, 1940)

Divorcee (1934) with Fred Astaire and Ginger Rogers, and *Gold Diggers of 1935.*

One of her best giddy mother roles was in *My Man Godfrey,* as mother to Carole Lombard and Gail Patrick. Her "pet" was Mischa Auer, as an eccentric musician who hung about the house mostly to amuse Miss Brady, who managed to sustain the illusion throughout the film that she had no idea what was going on.

But only three years later, it was a serious mother role that won Alice Brady an Oscar as best supporting actress of 1938. The film was *In Old Chicago,* in which she played the mother of Tyrone Power— the Mrs. O'Leary whose cow is traditionally blamed for starting the Chicago fire.

But she made only a few more films. Her last was

Young Mr. Lincoln, made in 1939, the same year in which she died.

Billie Burke, the third of our trio of Bs, is undoubtedly best remembered now as Mrs. Topper, the vague but agreeable wife of the mousy man who inherits a couple of fun-loving ghosts. Remarkably, there were only three films in the Topper series, but they were most successful and served to identify Roland Young and Billie Burke as a funny duo.

But she had been around for a good many years before that, making her name first on Broadway, then in silent films. As flighty as Miss Boland or Miss Brady, she nevertheless had a fragile charm that somehow made her more likable, even when she played silly women.

A slight change of pace for her was *The Young in*

48

In Old Chicago. Alice Faye comforts Alice Brady in this scene. Miss Brady played Tyrone Power's mother and, of course, the big fire provided the big finish. (20th Century-Fox, 1938)

New Moon. Mary Boland and Jeanette MacDonald in a scene from one of the successful MacDonald-Eddy musicals. (MGM, 1940)

The Young in Heart. Billie Burke, Douglas Fairbanks, Jr., Roland Young, and Janet Gaynor were all after Minnie Dupree's money in this comedy. (United Artists, 1938)

Heart, in which she was one of a family of charming rogues out to bilk a dear old lady. She and Roland Young were the parents of Janet Gaynor and Douglas Fairbanks, Jr.

In 1942, she was back to playing straight giddy mother, having been handed a choice role. This was in *The Man Who Came to Dinner,* in which egotistical lecturer Monty Woolley takes over the small-town home of Grant Mitchell and Billie Burke and in time aids their teenage daughter in running away from home. The same year, Miss Burke was Bette Davis's invalid mother in a generally undistinguished drama called *In This Our Life.* And still in that busy year, she was Joan Crawford's flighty, helpless mother in a pointless comedy titled *They All Kissed the Bride.*

Her career went downhill after that, but in 1950 she was back in a successful film, *Father of the Bride,* with Spencer Tracy, Joan Bennett, and Elizabeth Taylor. Miss Burke was mother of the groom (Don Taylor) and the film was a big enough hit to warrant a follow-up the next year, *Father's Little Dividend.* Once again Billie was around, as Elizabeth Taylor's mother-in-law.

Two more actresses whose last names begin with B merit considerable attention: Fay Bainter and Beulah Bondi.

Fay Bainter, with stage experience behind her, was in Hollywood by the early 1930s. In three years, she hit the jackpot, appearing in a film in which she was both mother and daughter. This was Leo McCarey's excellent examination of the practical problems of old age, *Make Way for Tomorrow.* Miss Bainter, married to Thomas Mitchell, is forced to

White Banners. Fay Bainter, center, in one of her few starring roles. With her are Kay Johnson and Claude Rains. (Warner Brothers, 1938)

Young Tom Edison. Mickey Rooney was the young
inventor-to-be and Fay Bainter was his loyal Mom.
(MGM, 1940)

take in her aged mother-in-law (Beulah Bondi)
when her husband's parents have to be split up as
the only sensible means of sharing the costs of supporting them. Victor Moore, as Miss Bondi's husband, is shipped off to another child. The pressures
of having a mother-in-law around are aptly drama-
tized, particularly in the clashes between Miss Bainter and Miss Bondi, and even those involving Barbara Read as Miss Bainter's rebellious daughter.

A year later, Miss Bainter did even better: she
played mother to Bette Davis in *Jezebel,* a widely
acclaimed film about an iron-whimmed Southern belle
who wrecks several lives. Both Miss Davis and Miss
Bainter were nominated for Academy Awards for their
performances.

All told, 1938 was a good Fay Bainter year. She
also played another mother role—this time a leading role, opposite Claude Rains—in *White Banners,*
for which she was nominated as best actress. Thus,
she was competing in two categories in the same
year. Bette Davis won the best actress Oscar for
Jezebel, and Fay Bainter won the best supporting
award for the same film.

Perhaps influenced by the sermonlike quality of
White Banners, Miss Bainter developed a kind of
spiritual style to her work. One could almost hear
muted organ music every time she delivered a sup-
posedly profound line. But she was fine and down
to earth, as was virtually everyone else, in *Our
Town,* the 1940 film based on Thornton Wilder's
play. This time she was young William Holden's
mother, and Beulah Bondi, who played Fay Bainter's
mother-in-law in *Make Way For Tomorrow,* was the
mother of Martha Scott, the girl next door.

Miss Bainter went on playing mothers, some of them amusing, others heavily dramatic. She was in *Mother Carey's Chickens, Yes, My Darling Daughter, Daughters Courageous,* and *Young Tom Edison.* In the last-named one she was the mother of the famed inventor, played by Mickey Rooney. She played Rooney's mother again in *The Human Comedy,* in 1943.

She also appeared as friend-sidekick-sympathizer in such varied movies as *Journey for Margaret, Woman of the Year,* and *June Bride.* She was a mother again in *Three Is a Family,* a comedy; and in the 1945 version of *State Fair,* she was Jeanne Crain's mom.

There was about Miss Bainter an air of breeding, sort of Hollywood Classic Bitch mellowed by mother-

The Trail of the Lonesome Pine. Beulah Bondi shows concern over her injured son (Henry Fonda). The others are Fred MacMurray, Robert Barrat, Sylvia Sidney, and Fred Stone. (Paramount, 1936)

Beulah Bondi. She played mothers in so many costume movies one might almost expect to see her dressed this way on the street.

hood. This didn't hurt when she had to shift to comedy mothers (as in *The Secret Life of Walter Mitty,* with Danny Kaye), but it typed her as an urban or possibly small-town parent—never a rural one.

The rural, frontier, or farm mother was not beyond the ken of Beulah Bondi, perhaps the most versatile of mother actresses. She could shift from city to ranch, from kindly to sinister, from heavy drama to light comedy. There was also in her playing a flair for hinting at religious fanaticism, and this too served her well.

It came in handy, indeed, in one of her first films, *Rain* (1932), starring Joan Crawford. Miss Bondi played the grimly pious wife of the Bible-thumping missionary, Walter Huston.

In 1936, she had a splendid mother role in *The Trail of the Lonesome Pine,* a drama of hillbilly feuding. She was the mother of Henry Fonda, whose girl (Sylvia Sidney) became smitten by city slicker Fred MacMurray. The same year, she was in *The Gorgeous Hussy* (Joan Crawford), playing the backwoods-bred wife of Andrew Jackson (Lionel Barrymore).

For a time, Miss Bondi almost made a full-time career of playing James Stewart's movie mother. It's possible that producers, in their endless crap-shooting attempts to anticipate public tastes, felt Beulah Bondi was the right "type" to be Stewart's mother.

In any case, it kept her working. In *Of Human Hearts* (1938) she was the widow of Walter Huston

Track of the Cat. Robert Mitchum confronts Teresa Wright while his mother, Beulah Bondi, looks on disapprovingly. (Warner Brothers, 1954)

making every sacrifice to send James Stewart through school and into medical practice. In *Vivacious Lady,* the same year, she was a less sympathetic mother, faking heart palpitations to help turn Stewart against his nightclub-entertainer wife, Ginger Rogers.

Her role was smaller in *Mr. Smith Goes to Washington,* in 1939. She was Ma Smith, serene and kindly, never doubting for a moment that her boy (Stewart again) could clean all those crooks out of the Senate. She was widowed, understanding, and reliable again in *It's a Wonderful Life* (1946), once more with James Stewart as her son.

Down through the years, she played an assortment of supporting roles, sometimes as mother, sometimes as meddler. As mentioned in passing, she was Martha Scott's mother in *Our Town.* She played Fred MacMurray's mom in *Remember the Night.* She supported Irene Dunne and Cary Grant in *Penny Serenade,* was a mother again in *Our Hearts Were Young*

and Gay, was warm-hearted in *On Borrowed Time,* unhinged in *The Snake Pit,* lovable in *So Dear to My Heart,* wasted in *Latin Lovers.*

Beulah Bondi was probably at her best playing a sanctimonious, bitter woman whose venom is barely controlled. In 1954 she had one of her strongest roles in *Track of the Cat,* an unusual outdoor drama with Robert Mitchum, Tab Hunter, and Teresa Wright. Miss Bondi was a pious old battle-axe, disgusted with her whiskey-slurping husband, resentful of her younger son's weakness, jealous of his plans to marry. She had a marvelous time, spitting out invective, demeaning her own grown sons, and delivering one of those lines that always sounded peculiarly hers: "Don't blaspheme."

So she went, through the 1950s and into the 1960s. Altogether she appeared in just over fifty movies, was still acting, though less frequently, in her seventies.

The Stratton Story. Agnes Moorehead is trying to decide whether to let her son (James Stewart) become a ball player. At left is Frank Morgan. (MGM, 1949)

She did not, however, have a monopoly on good mother roles. Another fine stage actress who has left a lasting impression over the years is Agnes Moorehead, who first went to Hollywood as part of Orson Welles's Mercury Theater group in 1941.

Her first movie role was as the mother of Charles Foster Kane in the brilliant Welles film, *Citizen Kane.* Stern, ambitious for her young son, she gives him up at a tender age (after she inherits a fortune) to be educated abroad. Although she appears only briefly in the film, her performance is a haunting one. In her next movie, *The Magnificent Ambersons,* also for Welles, she was Aunt Fanny, a bitter spinster, ungiving and unloved. This time she got an Oscar nomination (but not the award) and recognition by the New York film critics as best actress of 1942.

For the next few years, Miss Moorehead kept ticking off neat jobs as meddling governesses, gossips, bitchy wives, and dried-up maiden aunts.

She turned up as Jane Wyman's cold aunt in *Johnny Belinda,* then as James Stewart's mother in *The Stratton Story.* She was Richard Basehart's hysterical mother in *Fourteen Hours,* a good drama about

a disturbed man (Basehart) on the brink of suicide. She was grumpily lovable as Captain Andy's wife in the 1951 remake of *Show Boat.* She had three daughters in *Those Redheads from Seattle,* a mishmash about the gold rush. She was Dan Dailey's mom in *Meet Me in Las Vegas;* and the mother of Genghis Khan (played by John Wayne, yet) in *The Conqueror.* She played a dowager queen—Alec Guinness's mother—in *The Swan;* and Montgomery Clift's mother in *Raintree County.* She even played the mother of Jesse and Frank James in a 1953 rehash of that western standby, this time solemnly titled *The True Story of Jesse James.*

At the opposite end of the spectrum was Rosemary DeCamp, who spent a good part of her career playing agreeable, vapid mothers to an assortment of stars. She was James Cagney's mom in *Yankee Doodle Dandy,* June Allyson's in *Strategic Air Command.*

Typical of her roles was the one in a 1951 Doris Day and Gordon MacRae musical, *On Moonlight Bay.* With Leon Ames barking around as the stern Papa, à la Clarence Day, Miss DeCamp was restricted to urging her son to finish his cereal and looking mildly concerned whenever Doris's romance hit a bump in the road.

Of all her thirty-odd films, it is difficult to remember her saying anything more provocative than "Yes, dear." This kind of sweetness may have fed the egos of male chauvinists of the time, but it did little to make the public sit up and take much notice of mothers on the screen.

On Moonlight Bay. Rosemary DeCamp was Doris Day's mother in this musical. Between them is Mary Wickes, the cook. Leon Ames, the father, is at left. (Warner Brothers, 1951)

Far more effective were actresses Like Lucille Watson, whose name is not as well known as her face. Miss Watson, a handsome, Canadian-born actress, had an aura of good breeding that was one of her strongest assets in numerous roles on the screen.

In 1939, she made life difficult for Carole Lombard, who had married her son, James Stewart, in *Made for Each Other.* Mother Watson had higher hopes for Jimmy and wasn't about to let Carole forget it in this enjoyable domestic drama.

She was even more at home in *Waterloo Bridge,* in 1940, a teary wartime drama with Vivien Leigh and Robert Taylor. She was Taylor's tea-sipping Mum, a lady down to her cushy Oriental rugs. Taylor and Miss Leigh, a chorus girl in London, have a whirlwind romance, then he's off to war and promptly reported missing in action. Hard put to make ends meet, Vivien takes to whoring and is a proper pro by the time Taylor turns up (surprise!) alive. Blinded by love to the change in her, Robert takes Vivien home to Mum, still too much a lady to slam the door, but too much a mother to encourage a revival of the romance. Miss Leigh considerately solves Mother Watson's dilemma by diving off Waterloo Bridge.

Later in the war (1943) Lucille Watson was a somewhat more compassionate, but equally regal, mother in *Watch on the Rhine.* She was Bette Davis's mother this time, a gracious type who suddenly has to put up with a son-in-law up to his ears in the anti-Nazi underground, a house guest who plays footsie with the Gestapo, and a few less cosmic

Waterloo Bridge. Classic confrontation between bride-to-be Vivien Leigh and future mother-in-law Lucille Watson. (MGM, 1940)

Watch on the Rhine. Lucille Watson, left, was a stalwart to Bette Davis and Donald Woods (right). Seated is Bette's husband in the film, Paul Lukas. (Warner Brothers, 1943)

complications. But she and the cause of Freedom come through with flying colors.

Shortly after the war, Miss Watson was Gene Tierney's high-born mother in *The Razor's Edge,* a Somerset Maugham tale of love and strife among the cognoscenti. And she was no less a blueblood in *Never Say Goodbye* (1946), *Ivy* (1947), *Julia Misbehaves* (1948), or *Harriet Craig* (1950), the last a remake of *Craig's Wife,* with Joan Crawford in the title role. Not the least of her claims to our attention is the fact that in 1945 she played Nick Charles's (William Powell) mother in *The Thin Man Goes Home,* the swan song of that series.

But the mother of all movie mothers—and almost invariably the heavy of any movie she appeared in—was the magnificent Gladys Cooper, who could impale her victims with a sneer of a flawlessly delivered line.

There is a story about Miss Cooper that had little to do with her acting career, except that it may offer a clue to her imperious personality. She was once a guest, so the story goes, at a garden party in England, when a breathless woman gushed up to her, presuming previous acquaintance, and proceeded to chat away. When Miss Cooper's cool manner finally got through to her, the offended woman whined, accusingly: "Why, Miss Cooper, you don't remember me, do you?"

"No, my dear, I don't," replied the actress. "And it's *your* fault."

British to the core, Miss Cooper was nevertheless familiar to American audiences through many roles,

Now Voyager. Gladys Cooper is near death in this scene. Mary Wickes, left, and Bette Davis, the dying woman's daughter, hover over her. (Warner Brothers, 1942)

home for more bitter repartee with her cold-hearted Mama, after which Miss Cooper expires, leaving Bette with new feelings of guilt.

Gladys Cooper continued to dominate her fellow players (wherever the script allowed) in *Love Letters* (1945), *Valley of Decision* (1945), *The Green Years* (1946), and *Homecoming* (1948). In *Valley of Decision* she was Greer Garson's employer; in *Mrs. Parkington,* she was Miss Garson's haughty mother.

In 1958, she got another mother role worthy of her talents. This was in *Separate Tables* in which she portrayed a mother (to Deborah Kerr) even more domineering, more spirit-crushing, more hateful than she had been in *Now, Voyager.* Holding firmly to her homely daughter's reins, refusing the terrified creature any freedom of will or thought, she turned Deborah into a dependent invalid, unable to defy her mother in anything. The film, incidentally, won Oscars for David Niven and Wendy Hiller, but Miss Cooper went unheralded.

In 1964, at the age of 76, Gladys Cooper was

most memorable as granite-willed mothers, or other equally forbidding relatives and in-laws.

She was properly icy to Joan Fontaine in *Rebecca,* in which Miss Cooper played Laurence Olivier's sister. That same year (1940) she was Dennis Morgan's snobbish Philadelphia Main Line mother in *Kitty Foyle,* opposed to her son's interest in working girl Ginger Rogers.

It was in 1942, however, that Gladys Cooper reached the heights of classic-bitchy movie motherhood. The latest of a long list of mothers to give Bette Davis a hard time, she outclassed them all in *Now Voyager.*

Miss Cooper's blue blood was transplanted to Boston's Back Bay, where she reigned supreme over a Victorian household whose most pathetic feature was the repressed daughter, played by Bette. With the help of a sympatico psychiatrist (Claude Rains) Bette escapes the cocoon and is transformed into a sophisticated woman capable of winning the love (if not the marriage vows) of Paul Henreid. Bette returns

Valley of Decision. Greer Garson was a domestic servant in this one, and Gladys Cooper was the matriarch. (MGM, 1945)

Separate Tables. One of Gladys Cooper's most frightening roles was in this drama. Deborah Kerr was the cowering daughter. (United Artists, 1958)

seen in another fine mother role, albeit a lighter one. More elegant than ever, she was the patient, gracious mother of Professor Henry Higgins (Rex Harrison) in *My Fair Lady.* It's interesting to note, by the way, how smoothly an actress associated with heavy dramatic roles slipped into this somewhat frothier part in a musical.

An American mother-type of considerable ability but little recognition was Anne Revere. After a number of unimportant roles in the early 1940s, she got two good mother parts in 1944. In *The Song of Bernadette,* she was the mother of Jennifer Jones, who heard voices. In *National Velvet,* her daughter was little Elizabeth Taylor, who was in love with horses. Miss Revere won a best supporting actress Oscar for the latter film

She was Anne Baxter's mother in *Sunday Dinner for a Soldier* (1945) and, in a better part, Gregory Peck's understanding Mom in *Gentlemen's Agreement* (1947).

Four years later, she had a small but worthwhile role in *A Place in the Sun,* the George Stevens version of Dreiser's *An American Tragedy.* She was Montgomery Clift's strict, religion-obsessed mother and, by inference, the cause of Clift's inner turmoil.

Jo Van Fleet, another actress of admirable skill, has also given us a few mothers worth recalling. She was Susan Hayward's mother in that actress's flamboyant portrayal of hard-drinking singer Lillian Roth in the 1956 film, *I'll Cry Tomorrow.* The year before that, Miss Van Fleet was hauntingly effective as James Dean's mother in *East of Eden.* And in 1967, she had a brief but moving part as Paul Newman's dying mother in *Cool Hand Luke.*

Judith Anderson, a gifted actress who has been equally at home on stage or screen, lent her substantial presence to a number of films, sometimes as a mother, usually as a villain. She first drew attention as Mrs. Danvers, the housekeeper in *Rebecca* (1940).

In *All Through the Night* (1941) she was working with Nazi agent Conrad Veidt in New York but ran afoul of gambler Humphrey Bogart, whose patriotism, it seems, superseded his lawlessness. But in 1943, Miss Anderson was on the good side, as an anti-Nazi Norwegian fighter in *Edge of Darkness,* with Errol Flynn and Ann Sheridan. Neither of these war-time films, so blatantly propagandistic, did much to enhance Judith Anderson's stature, but she fared better in *King's Row,* a murky drama of sin and evil in small-town America.

Unhappily, this fine player got trapped in a series of potboilers unworthy of her gifts (*Lady Scarface, Tycoon, The Red House*) and usually portraying all-too-obvious menaces. But there were bright spots, too, as Vincent Price's rich bitch mistress in *Laura;* and as Robert Mitchum's mother in *Pursued* (1947).

In *Salome* (1953) she was Rita Hayworth's bloodthirsty mother, urging Rita to demand John the Baptist's head. A few years later (1956) she was one of an army of vaguely biblical characters in Cecil B. DeMille's remake of *The Ten Commandments.*

One of her best mother roles came from the stage.

National Velvet. Anne Revere is the contemplative mother here. Donald Crisp was father, and the daughter was young Elizabeth Taylor. (MGM, 1944)

59

I'll Cry Tomorrow. Susan Hayward was the hard-drinking singer and Jo Van Fleet her tearful mother. (MGM, 1956)

Salome. Hard-hearted Judith Anderson had no compunctions about asking her daughter to demand John the Baptist's head. With her above is Arnold Moss. (Columbia, 1953)

In *Cat on a Hot Tin Roof,* she was cast as Big Mama, Burl Ives's dying wife and the mother of Paul Newman.

Some pretty big stars have also, from time to time, taken on mother roles, often with most gratifying results.

Angela Lansbury, for example, was a most horrendous mother to robotlike Laurence Tierney in the film version of Richard Condon's hair-raising novel, *The Manchurian Candidate.* But she was less fortunate in three other mother parts: as Carroll Baker's in *Harlow* (1965), as Warren Beatty's in *All Fall Down* (1962); and as Elvis Presley's in *Blue Hawaii* (1961).

Katharine Hepburn, that most durable of glamorous actresses, was Elizabeth Taylor's ruthless moth-er-in-law in *Suddenly Last Summer* (1959). In 1962, she was the mother of Jason Robards and Dean Stockwell in Eugene O'Neill's epic drama, *Long Day's Journey into Night.* Five years later, with Spencer Tracy for the last time, she was Katharine Houghton's gutsy mother in *Guess Who's Coming to Dinner.* And in 1968, when she won her third Academy Award, it was as the regal mother of an odd assortment of sons in *The Lion in Winter.*

Rosalind Russell, who has represented virtually every career known to woman in films, turned mother in *Gypsy* (1962), raucously urging Natalie Wood to "sing out, Louise." In the same year, Miss Russell played a rather less appealing mother in *Five Finger Exercise,* in which she hankered for her son's tutor—as did her son in the story. And she was

Harlow. Angela Lansbury, holding the tray, was Jean Harlow's mother in this bio-film. Carroll Baker played the blond bombshell, and Raf Vallone, right, was also in it. (Paramount, 1965)

Suddenly Last Summer. Katharine Hepburn is urging
Montgomery Clift to get busy with her daughter-in-
law's lobotomy. The victimized daughter-in-law was
Elizabeth Taylor. (Columbia, 1959)

Guess Who's Coming to Dinner. Sidney Poitier was the dinner guest, Spencer Tracy and Katharine Hepburn the parents of the girl he loved. (Columbia, 1967)

Five Finger Exercise. Rosalind Russell and Richard Beymer were mother and son, both interested in his tutor. (Columbia, 1962)

Lolita. Sue Lyon kisses her stepfather, James Mason, goodnight. At right is Mama Shelley Winters. (MGM, 1962)

I Remember Mama. Irene Dunne was the level-headed mother and Philip Dorn, left, was the father. Next to him stands their oldest daughter, Barbara Bel Geddes. (RKO, 1948)

Inside Daisy Clover. Ruth Gordon was Natalie Wood's eccentric mother in this Hollywood yarn. (Warner Brothers, 1966)

Mrs. Wiggs of the Cabbage Patch. Pauline Lord played the title role, and Zasu Pitts was the resident spinster. (Paramount, 1934)

in yet another stage adaptation, *Oh, Dad, Poor Dad, Mama's Hung You in the Closet and I'm Feelin' So Sad* (1967), a film about as tedious as its title.

Shelley Winters was one of the delights of *Lolita* (1962), playing the blowsy mother of the famous Nabokov "nymphet." She was more repulsive as the mother of a blind girl (Elizabeth Hartman) who fell in love with a black (Sidney Poitier) in *A Patch of Blue* (1965), but she won a best supporting actress Oscar for her splendid effort.

Wild in the Streets (1968) was an imaginative drama about a young rock singer (Christopher Jones) who becomes president of the United States and throws everyone over thirty into concentration camps—including his own mother, played by Shelley Winters. And in 1970, she was Ma Barker in a gory mess appropriately titled *Bloody Mama.*

Irene Dunne, long after her Cary Grant and Charles Boyer periods, gave us two charming mother performances: as William Powell's patient wife and the mother of that brood of redheads in *Life with Father* (1948); and, in the same year, as the sensible and devoted mother of Barbara Bel Geddes in *I Remember Mama.*

Ruth Gordon, that delightful pixie, was seventy when she played Natalie Wood's eccentric mother in *Inside Daisy Clover* (1966). Three years later she was outrageously funny as the tushy-pinching

Sing, You Sinners. Elizabeth Patterson bears down on her three bruised sons, Donald O'Connor, Fred Mac-Murray, and Bing Crosby. (Paramount, 1938)

mother of George Segal in *Where's Poppa?*

And there are still more actresses who have captured our attention (and/or affection) over the years in a full spectrum of mother roles. They rate at least a mention:

Pauline Lord in *Mrs. Wiggs of the Cabbage Patch* (1934), ruling benevolently over a batch of mischief makers.

May Robson as Clark Gable's mother in *Wife Versus Secretary* (1936), planting the seeds of doubt in daughter-in-law Myrna Loy's mind about Gable's relations with Jean Harlow. And also as Janet Gaynor's crusty old grandmother in *A Star Is Born* (1937).

Scrawny Elizabeth Patterson, torn between appreciation of her hard-working son (Fred MacMurray) and affection for her wastrel son (Bing Crosby) in *Sing, You Sinners* (1938).

The inimitable Maria Ouspenskaya, firmly pouring cold water on Irene Dunne's hopes of marrying Charles Boyer in *Love Affair* (1939). But she was

Escape. This time, Robert Taylor was trying to get his mother, Alla Nazimova, left, out of Germany. Taylor's co-star was Norma Shearer. (MGM, 1940)

a vastly more compassionate mother to James Stewart in *The Mortal Storm* (1940).

Alla Nazimova, long inactive star of the silents, back to play Robert Taylor's ailing mother in Nazi Germany in *Escape* (1940), with Norma Shearer. The next year, she was Tyrone Power's mother in *Blood and Sand.*

In another anti-Nazi film, *Four Sons* (1940), Eugenie Leontovich was the indomitable mother of Don Ameche, Alan Curtis, Robert Lowry, and George Ernest.

Ina Claire, as Dorothy McGuire's dying mother in *Claudia* (1943), with Robert Young as the understanding son-in-law.

Ethel Barrymore's glowing performance as Cary Grant's mother in prewar London squalor as represented by Richard Llewellyn's story, *None but the Lonely Heart* (1944).

Mady Christian's loyal wife and mother in the Arthur Miller drama about wartime profiteering, *All My Sons* (1948).

Katina Paxinou in a classic mother role updated by Eugene O'Neill as *Mourning Becomes Electra* (1947).

Anne Seymour as wife to politician Broderick Crawford and devoted mother to John Derek in *All the King's Men* (1949).

Gertrude Lawrence as Tennessee Williams's garrulous, day-dreaming mother (of Jane Wyman) in a largely ineffective screen translation of *The Glass Menagerie* (1950).

The Mortal Storm. No amount of Nazi terror could defeat Maria Ouspenskaya, right, mother of James Stewart. The young lady is Margaret Sullavan. (MGM, 1940)

Four Sons. Eugenie Leontovich stoically receives a
Nazi medal for her dead son, Alan Curtis, who had
turned Nazi. Another son, Don Ameche, was a loyal
Czech who also got killed. (20th Century-Fox, 1940)

None but the Lonely Heart. Ethel Barrymore was Cary
Grant's spunky mother in this warm drama. At right is
Barry Fitzgerald. (RKO, 1944)

All My Sons. Despite Edward G. Robinson's war profiteering, Mady Christian (center) was loyal to him. The son at left is Burt Lancaster. (Universal, 1948)

Mourning Becomes Electra. Katina Paxinou, clinging to Michael Redgrave, was the mother in this film. The man at left is Kirk Douglas. (RKO, 1947)

All the King's Men. Anne Seymour braces herself as Broderick Crawford is about to slap their son, John Derek. At right is John Ireland. (Columbia, 1949)

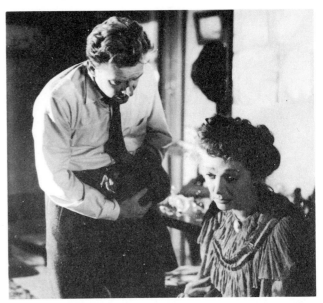

The Glass Menagerie. Arthur Kennedy and Gertrude Lawrence in a scene from the film version of Tennessee Williams's play. (Warner Brothers, 1950)

Sweet Bird of Youth. Mildred Dunnock played good mother roles by both Arthur Miller and Tennessee Williams. This one is the latter's play, and Paul Newman is seen with her. (MGM, 1962)

I Want You. Mildred Dunnock and Farley Granger were in this Samuel Goldwyn drama made during the Korean War. (RKO, 1951)

My Son John. Robert Walker was the crypto-Commie, Helen Hayes the patriotic American mother in this McCarthy era film. (Paramount, 1952)

The Importance of Being Ernest. Dame Edith Evans made a magnificent Lady Bracknell in this British-made Oscar Wilde comedy. (Universal, 1952)

The Rose Tattoo. Anna Magnani was the fiery Italian mother and Burt Lancaster her uncouth lover in this lively film. (Paramount, 1955)

Marty. Ernest Borgnine, in the title role, had a rough time with his mother, Esther Minciotti. (United Artists, 1955)

Mildred Dunnock as the long-suffering wife of Willy Loman (Fredric March) in Arthur Miller's finest work, *Death of a Salesman* (1951), as well as mother roles in some less important films.

Helen Hayes as a patriotic mother who can't bear the thought that her son (Robert Walker) is a Communist, in the McCarthy-era film, *My Son John* (1952).

Dame Edith Evans as the terrifying Lady Bracknell in *The Importance of Being Ernest* (1952). When her daughter's suitor, under cross-examination, confesses reluctantly that he has neither mother nor father living, Lady Bracknell snorts: "To lose one parent is regrettable. To lose both seems careless."*

Anna Magnani's fiery version of maternal love in *The Rose Tattoo* (1955). When daughter Marisa Pavan insists that her new beau is a Catholic, Mama Magnani retorts: "He don't look Catholic."

Esther Minciotti, who kept urging her son (Ernest Borgnine) to get married—until he decided to do just that—in *Marty* (1955).

Wendy Hiller's fine performance as Dean Stockwell's loving but possessive mother in *Sons and Lovers* (1960).

Ann Shoemaker's strong portrayal of the formidable matriarch, Sara Delano Roosevelt, in *Sunrise at Campobello* (1960).

Selena Royle as the gentle grandmother of an orphaned boy in *The Green Years* (1946).

Claudette Colbert, mother to Troy Donahue, in a generally soapy drama called *Parrish* (1961).

Joan Crawford, mother to Ann Blyth in a highly

---

* A rare instance of a screenplay's dialogue being funnier than that of the original playwright, in this case Oscar Wilde.

Sons and Lovers. Wendy Hiller, center, was the mother, Trevor Howard, left, the father, and Dean Stockwell, the son. (20th Century Fox, 1960)

Sunrise at Campobello. Ann Shoemaker, as Sara Delano Roosevelt, comforts young Anna (Zina Bethune) as Eleanor Roosevelt (Greer Garson) looks on. (Warner Brothers, 1960)

The Green Years. Selena Royle receives her orphaned grandson (Dean Stockwell) in the fine version of A. J. Cronin's novel. (MGM, 1946)

Parrish. Troy Donahue is the son, Dean Jagger and Claudette Colbert the parents. (Warner Brothers, 1961)

Mildred Pierce. Ann Blyth dances with Zachary Scott as her mother, Joan Crawford, looks on contentedly. Things got heavier later. (Warner Brothers, 1945)

Come Blow Your Horn. That's Molly Picon who can't believe what she just heard on the phone. She was Frank Sinatra's mother in this comedy. (Paramount, 1963)

successful drama, *Mildred Pierce* (1945).

Molly Picon as the All-American Jewish mother in *Come Blow Your Horn* (1963).

Ethel Merman, a boisterous mother to a nutty Dick Shawn in *It's a Mad, Mad, Mad, Mad World* (1963).

Geraldine Page's funny interpretation of the mother of Peter Kastner in *You're a Big Boy Now* (1964).

Kate Reid's slattern of a mother to Natalie Wood in the steamy tale, *This Property Is Condemned* (1966).

Eileen Heckart's overprotective mother to a blind boy (Edward Albert) in *Butterflies Are Free* (1972), which won her an Oscar.

And finally, that old favorite Classic Bitch, Binnie Barnes, transformed (39 years after her screen debut) into a giddy but delightful mother to Liv Ullman in *Forty Carats* (1973).

Mothers of the screen, we salute you!

It's a Mad, Mad, Mad, Mad World. Spencer Tracy just knocked Ethel Merman down. She played Dick Shawn's mother. (United Artists, 1963)

You're a Big Boy Now. Geraldine Page, center, was a scatterbrained mother in this comedy. (Seven Arts, 1964)

Butterflies Are Free. Eileen Heckart and Goldie Hawn are arguing over the latter's interest in the former's son. (Columbia, 1972)

Forty Carats. Binnie Barnes, second from right, was
Liv Ullman's mother in this comedy. Holding Liv's
hand is Edward Albert. (Columbia, 1973)

3

Bosom Buddies

During Hollywood's halcyon days, it was an immutable part of plotting logic in countless films that the leading lady needed a friend. Said friend—female, of course—would be on hand to give out advice, listen to the heroine's troubles, butt in to help straighten out romantic misunderstandings, tell the thoughtless hero where to get off, soothe the sobbing heroine, or comment (like some movieland Greek Chorus) on the silly actions of the film's stars.

She could perform some or all of these functions within a loose framework of character delineation. She might be a frustrated husband hunter herself; she could be a pal who's been through the mill, growing wiser if not sadder; or she might be one of those man haters through whom the American puritan ethic sometimes expressed itself. She could be savant or scatterbrain, kin or kibitzer, roommate or working colleague, sister or secretary, shallow or shrewd, cheerful or churlish. Age, somehow, didn't really matter.

But one prerequisite was absolutely essential: she must never be as attractive as the star. She could be fat or thin, homely or cute, shy or brassy; but she must never be regarded as a serious threat to the aspirations of the leading lady. Some stars may even have had clauses in their contracts to that effect.

Even with these rigid basic restrictions, there was enough leeway to allow a number of variations on

the Bosom Buddy role, and quite a few actresses of less than star stature were able to operate comfortably within the rules and work fairly regularly.

In romantic comedies, the Buddy was often in a position to speak the irreverent thoughts that were beneath the dignity of the female star. In more serious stories, the Buddy must be sympathetic and understanding, and might be instrumental in solving the problem faced by the heroine—sometimes even by sacrificing her own wishes, but never to the extent that would cost the star the audience's good wishes.

In musicals, where producers preferred to leave things neat and tidy by the final fadeout, the Buddy might be thrown a bone—some Hugh Herbert or Jack Haley to link arms with, thereby implying to the drones in the darkened theater that even unglamorous females have a chance at Romance.

On those occasions (and it happened) when the Bosom Buddy was assigned to the male star, caution must be taken to keep it on a platonic level. And even if the hero's confidante harbored a crush on him, either he must be blissfully unaware of this or he must be true enough to the star to avoid reciprocating it or even acknowledging it.

For all these ground rules, Hollywood did manage, for a period of several decades, to grind out a procession of such roles. Perhaps more important, enough capable actresses turned up to bring life to the Bosom Buddy roles.

Dark Victory. Geraldine Fitzgerald was the essence of Bosom Buddyhood to soon-to-go-blind Bette Davis in this drama. (Warner Brothers, 1939)

To illustrate the variety of styles and personalities involved, let's take a couple of examples, each markedly different from the other: Geraldine Fitzgerald and Una Merkel.

Miss Fitzgerald, Irish born and a stage and film actress in Britain before she invaded Hollywood, got the ideal Buddy role in one of her first films: *Dark Victory,* in 1939, then as now a favorite film with Bette Davis fans.

It was an unabashed tearjerker in which Bette had a brain tumor that even brilliant brain surgeon George Brent couldn't exorcise. Bette, a Long Island socialite with not much to do but worry about her tumor, had a secretary (Miss Fitzgerald) to help her. And it's a good thing, too, because a girl in that condition needs a friend and Geraldine was certainly that. She was sympathetic understanding personified.

After Bette goes through her bitter, what's-the-use-of-anything period, and comes to terms with her impending demise, it is Geraldine again who stands by, a veritable fortress of loyalty. Bette even allows surgeon Brent (by now her husband) to go off to Washington on business when she knows that death is closing in on her. But Geraldine is there to the end, helping the nearly blind Bette get to bed for the last time.

The picture was a smash hit and although it was indisputably Miss Davis's triumph, there was enough praise left over to cover Geraldine Fitzgerald as well, and it looked as if she might soon be a star on her own.

The same year, Miss Fitzgerald was seen in support of Laurence Olivier and Merle Oberon in *Wuthering Heights,* another successful film based on Emily Brontë's famous book. Geraldine was seen as Isabella, sister of David Niven (Edgar) and friend of Cathy (Merle). At one point in the film, Isabella, ignoring Cathy's warnings, marries Heathcliff (Olivier) only to learn that he still loves Cathy. In this film, Miss Fitzgerald was both friend to the heroine and pawn in the tragic love story. Like all the other principals,. she got good reviews and the film is still regarded with nostalgic pleasure by buffs.

Miss Fitzgerald's path seemed paved with tears. Before arriving in Hollywood, she had already appeared in a British film version of George Eliot's 1860 novel, *The Mill on the Floss,* in which adversity ran rampant. The film was released in the United States in 1939—the same year as *Dark Victory* and *Wuthering Heights.*

The following year, Miss Fitzgerald was again a loyal friend to a doomed woman. The film was *Till We Meet Again,* with George Brent and Merle Oberon in the leads. (Eight years earlier, as *One Way Passage,* it had been a big hit for William Powell and Kay Francis.) Merle had an incurable disease and Brent was on his way to prison. Geraldine was compassionate as all get-out, but there's no way to beat those odds.

Miss Fitzgerald, in those days when she was seemingly being groomed for stardom, played a few leads,

Broadway Melody of 1936. The perfect position for a Bosom Buddy: between the stars (Robert Taylor and Eleanor Powell) and a little bit below them. That's Una Merkel. (MGM, 1936)

True Confession. A good pal like Una Merkel was sometimes called upon to tell the heroine off. In this case it's Carole Lombard. (Paramount, 1937)

too, but always in B pictures: *A Child Is Born,* a maternity ward drama with Jeffrey Lynn; *Flight from Destiny,* with Thomas Mitchell; *Shining Victory,* in which she perished in a fire set by a psychotic rival.

In 1943, she was back with Bette Davis in *Watch on the Rhine,* Lillian Hellman's drama about resistance to the Nazis. Geraldine is married to the villain (George Coulouris) but in love with Bette's brother (Donald Woods). In the end, both Bette and Geraldine wind up manless.

In succeeding years, Miss Fitzgerald's acting talents were often wasted on bad films, although she burst out now and then with a good performance in a worthwhile one—in *The Pawnbroker* (1965) with Rod Steiger, for example—but for the most

part she was strapped into that understanding-friend-to-the-heroine harness that first brought attention to her.

Una Merkel was the antithesis of Geraldine Fitzgerald. She spent a lifetime playing sympathetic but wisecracking friends to leading ladies, in musicals and light comedies. Starting her Hollywood career as Lillian Gish's double, she was soon appearing on the screen in Bosom Buddy roles.

In the 1931 version of *The Maltese Falcon* (with Ricardo Cortez and Bebe Daniels) she was Effie, Sam Spade's loyal and efficient secretary. In *Forty Second Street* (1933) she was a worldly wise chorine who could squelch a wolf with a line like: "My, you have the busiest hands."

Her flat, somewhat nasal delivery made lines sound

funnier than they might coming from someone else. Plain looking enough to be a contrast to any glamorous leading lady, accepted by audiences as "real," Miss Merkel had no trouble working in films for a quarter of a century.

She was Eleanor Powell's pal in *Broadway Melody of 1936*, and again in *Born To Dance*. She was with Tracy and Harlow in *Riffraff* (1936) and with Gable and Harlow in *Saratoga* (1937). She was loyal to Carole Lombard in *True Confession* (1937) and sympathetic to James Stewart in *Destry Rides Again* (1939). She aided and abetted Crosby and Hope in *The Road to Zanzibar* (1941) and she had W. C. Fields to put up with in *The Bank Dick* (1940).

She occupied neither of the *Twin Beds* (1942) with Joan Bennett and George Brent, and she wasn't the bride in *The Bride Goes Wild* (1948), with June Allyson and Van Johnson. With Jane Powell and Vic Damone, she was in *Rich, Young, and Pretty* (1951) but the title, as usual, didn't refer to her.

So valuable and enduring a supporting actress was she that Miss Merkel appeared in two versions of *The Merry Widow*: once, with Jeanette MacDonald and Maurice Chevalier, in 1934; and again with Lana Turner and Fernando Lamas, in 1952.

After some seventy-five movies, she turned up on Broadway in a hit musical called *Take Me Along* (based on Eugene O'Neill's play, *Ah Wilderness*). Its·

Cain and Mabel. Ruth Donnelly, right, made sure David Carlyle didn't get too far with Marion Davies. After all, Marion's co-star was Clark Gable. (Warner Brothers, 1936)

cast was studded with stars like Jackie Gleason, Walter Pidgeon, and Robert Morse. But when the then fifty-six-year-old Una Merkel made her nightly first appearance a gasp of recognition swept the audience and won her a warm round of applause.

Distinctive and popular though she was, Una Merkel had plenty of competition in the Bosom Buddy field. Hollywood found ample use for the unglamorous, mildly sarcastic, usually funny female friend. Others who became familiar to audiences in the 1930s and 1940s include Ruth Donnelly, Patsy Kelly, Jean Dixon, Joan Davis, and Glenda Farrell.

Like other competent actresses, Ruth Donnelly was lost amid the opulent Busby Berkeley production numbers in films like *Footlight Parade* (1933). Still, she managed to make an impression in enough of her early movies to be kept busy. Typical of her roles was as Carole Lombard's fellow manicurist in *Hands Across the Table* (1935). She alternated between clucking romantically at Carole's interest in impractical Fred MacMurray, and letting Carole know that if she had any sense she'd go for wealthy Ralph Bellamy. She was an aide d'amour again in *Cain and Mabel* (1936), with Clark Gable and Marion Davies.

In the midst of a spate of routine B pictures, Ruth Donnelly landed a good part in what turned out to be a first-rate comedy. This was Warners' *A Slight Case of Murder*, in which she was the wife of a reformed gangster (Edward G. Robinson) who was bent on social climbing.

Despite its success, it was back to the Bs again (*Scatterbrain*, with Judy Canova and Alan Mowbray, *Rise and Shine*, with Jack Oakie and Linda Darnell) with an occasional role in a bigger picture, like *Mr. Deeds Goes to Town* and *Mr. Smith Goes to Washington*.

A year after the latter film, she was with W. C. Fields and Mae West in *My Little Chickadee*, a movie noteworthy for its teaming of these two unique stars, if nothing else. Fields is supposed to have written his own script, Miss West penned hers. Nobody, it seems, bothered about the supporting cast.

Not until 1945 did Ruth Donnelly have another role worthy of mention. That was in *The Bells of St. Mary's,* in which she and Ingrid Bergman were friendly nuns charmed by Bing Crosby. Eleven years after that (1956) she had another good-friend role—as Joan Crawford's brusque but warm-hearted landlady—in *Autumn Leaves.*

Holiday. Jean Dixon was a flawless friend to Katharine Hepburn in this comedy-with-a-message. (Columbia, 1938)

After she became a widow in 1958, she moved to New York, and in 1963, at the age of sixty-seven, was in a Broadway play, *The Riot Act.*

Although Jean Dixon's career was much shorter than Ruth Donnelly's, she managed to make an impression in several Bosom Buddy roles. In 1934, she was with Joan Crawford in *Sadie McKee.* Two years later, she was a pal to Myrna Loy in *To Mary with Love.*

Miss Dixon was Carole Lombard's loyal buddy in *Swing High, Swing Low,* when the male star was Fred MacMurray. And she was with Irene Dunne and Douglas Fairbanks, Jr., in *The Joy of Living.*

But perhaps her best role—and her last film— was in *Holiday* (1938), with Katharine Hepburn and Cary Grant. In this sly Philip Barry play, Miss Dixon was married to Edward Everett Horton. Both were warm, fun-loving, and devoted to Grant. But Miss Dixon in particular helped heiress Hepburn to appreciate Grant's nonconformist philosophy.

Another champion Bosom Buddy was the inimitable Patsy Kelly. She started on Broadway in 1931 in an Al Jolson musical, *The Wonder Bar*—and returned there four decades later in the nostalgic hit, *No, No, Nanette.*

Her film career began in 1933 in *Going Hollywood,* with Bing Crosby and Marion Davies. Shortly after that, she was signed by Hal Roach, whose past achievements had involved Harold Lloyd, the *Our Gang* comedies, and the teaming of Laurel and Hardy. Roach teamed Patsy Kelly with Thelma Todd to make a series of two-reel comedies that met with great success. After Miss Todd died in 1935, Patsy was teamed with Lyda Roberti for more of these comedy shorts, but Miss Roberti died, too, in 1938.

In the meantime, however, Patsy Kelly had established a wide reputation as a disarming comedienne. She was Jean Harlow's buddy in *The Girl from Missouri* (1934) and Ruby Keeler's in *Go into Your Dance* (1935).

In succeeding films, she was confidante to Ann Dvorak (*Thanks a Million*), Loretta Young (*Private Number*), Marion Davies again (*Page Miss Glory*), and Alice Faye (*Sing, Baby, Sing*).

In *Every Night at Eight*, Patsy was the third girl in a vocal trio (with Alice Faye and Frances Langford) trying to break into radio. Faye got the man (George Raft) and Kelly got the laughs. In *Wake Up and Live,* she was the wisecracking assistant to columnist Walter Winchell. In 1938, she was a domestic in the home of socialite Merle Oberon in *The Cowboy and the Lady.*

When she wasn't being the heroine's buddy, she was somebody's irreverent maid. In either case, her faintly Brooklynese inflection, her mobile face, and her deadpan delivery of lines calculated to deflate anyone's pomposity all combined to make Patsy Kelly a valuable asset to the casts of dozens of movies spread over some thirty years.

Similar to her in appeal, if not exactly in style, was Joan Davis. Another of those ladies who could turn an absence of glamor into an asset, she could modulate her voice to get a variety of funny readings out of mundane dialogue, she was an expert at the "take," and she specialized in handing

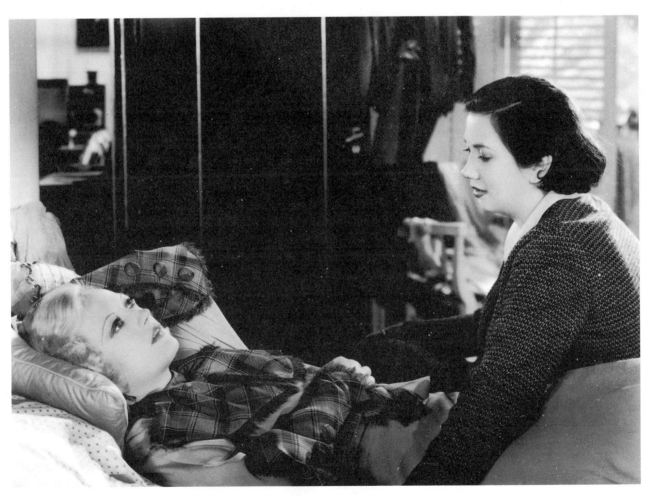

Going Hollywood. What's a buddy for, if not to listen to you when you're down and out? That's Patsy Kelly listening to Marion Davies. (MGM, 1933)

Thanks a Million. Dick Powell and Ann Dvorak were
hero and heroine, but Patsy Kelly, left, was along for
comradeship. (20th Century-Fox, 1935)

Sun Valley Serenade. Expert buddy Joan Davis and
Milton Berle were the comic leads in this musical.
The lady about to detrain was star Sonja Henie. (20th
Century-Fox, 1941)

out sensible advice to leading ladies, all the while masking her shrewdness with a kind of bungling air, somehow suggesting a Disney ugly duckling loose in a china shop.

The studio where she did most of her film work was 20th Century-Fox, and she back-stopped such box-office biggies as Sonja Henie, Alice Faye, Simone Simon, Linda Darnell, and both of the studio's money-making child stars, Shirley Temple and Jane Withers.

When she wasn't being some lovesick heroine's true-blue friend, she was teamed with a procession of male comedians: Leon Errol in *She Gets Her Man;* Jack Haley in *Make Mine Laughs;* Eddie Cantor in *Show Business;* Abbott and Costello in *Hold That Ghost.*

After some twenty years in movies, she moved into television with her own series, "I Married Joan," in which she was teamed with Jim Backus.

Another of the wise-cracking Bosom Buddies of the 1930s was Glenda Farrell, who paid her dues in supporting roles in those Busby Berkeley musicals. Miss Farrell, somewhat more caustic than most of the others, had a kind of passed-over Mae West quality to her personality.

Among her early films were *Little Caesar,* with Edward G. Robinson, and *I Am a Fugitive from a Chain Gang,* with Paul Muni, both in 1932.

Then came the musicals—*Gold Diggers of 1935, Go Into Your Dance, In Caliente, Gold Diggers of 1937.* Berkeley always had a platoon of fetching

Gold Diggers of 1937. Glenda Farrell, here flanked by Charles D. Brown and Osgood Perkins, was often on hand to aid and comfort heroines. (Warner Brothers, 1937)

chorines, doing military taps, saluting the flag, playing a gross of pianos, backs arched around harps, heads popping out of cannons, silhouetted against giant cog wheels symbolizing Industry, out-Ziegfelding Ziegfeld. It's a wonder that any individual personalities emerged from that busy background of pre-June Taylor dancers. But somehow they did, and Glenda Farrell was one of them.

Perhaps more than most of the others, she personified the gold digger of the era—wise to the ways of Broadway heels, determined to land a Sugar Daddy, ready with all the answers, if only someone would ask the questions. But it was always Ruby Keeler who became the star overnight, while Glenda and the other fortune-hunters fanned out to form a semicircle for the big closing production number.

But Miss Farrell was not to be overlooked. In 1937, Warners put her into a picture called *Smart Blonde,* in which she played a fast-talking, sardonic newspaper reporter named Torchy Blaine. It was successful enough to lead to a mini-series that lasted for half a dozen more Torchy Blaine films, with Glenda Farrell and Barton MacLane, the latter in a surprising departure from gangster roles.

In between, she still turned up aiding and abetting in such movies as *Breakfast for Two* (Barbara Stanwyck and Herbert Marshall, 1937), *Twin Beds* (Joan Bennett and George Brent, 1942), *Talk of the Town* (Jean Arthur and Cary Grant, 1942), and *Johnny Eager* (Lana Turner and Robert Taylor, 1942).

By 1948, she was reduced to such inanities as *Lulu Belle,* with Dorothy Lamour and George Montgomery, and in 1954 *Secret of the Incas,* with Charlton Heston and Nicole Maurey.

She had one good Bosom Buddy (Mature Sister Division) role in *Middle of the Night* (1959) with Fredric March and Kim Novak, in which she cautioned March against marrying the far-too-young Kim. After that, it was appearances in Elvis Presley musicals and Jerry Lewis comedies.

Even more winning—and more durable—was Joan Blondell, whose early Hollywood background was much the same as Glenda Farrell's, Patsy Kelly's, and Una Merkel's.

Blond, bright-eyed, and bubbling, Joan Blondell was impossible to resist. She was perhaps the classic example of the first-rate supporting player who never quite made it up that last rung to stardom.

She supported Barbara Stanwyck in *Illicit* and

Footlight Parade. Although James Cagney is interested in Claire Dodd, Joan Blondell is there to protect Ruby Keeler's interests. (Warner Brothers, 1933)

Night Nurse (1931). She was a friend in *My Past,* with Bebe Daniels and Ben Lyon (1931). She was Loretta Young's pal in *Big Business Girl,* with Ricardo Cortez, the same year. In 1932, she was one of a trio (Madge Evans and Ina Claire were the others) in *The Greeks Had a Word for Them.* It was trio time again in *Three on a Match,* with Bette Davis and Ann Dvorak.

Warners teamed her with Glenda Farrell for *Havana Widows, Travelling Saleslady,* and *Miss Pacific Fleet*—all Bs. She was the smiling loser in *Colleen,* with Ruby Keeler and Dick Powell, and again in *Stage Struck,* with Powell and Jeanne Madden.

By the early 1940s, she was one of the *Two Girls on Broadway* (with Lana Turner) and one of the *Three Girls about Town* (Janet Blair and Binnie Barnes), as well as part of another trio (with Ann Sothern and Margaret Sullavan) in *Cry Havoc.*

In 1944, she landed a meaty supporting role, as Aunt Cissy in *A Tree Grows in Brooklyn,* with James Dunn, Dorothy McGuire, and Peggy Ann Garner. But two years later, she was back to buddying: Greer Garson's chum in *Adventure,* with Clark Gable; Joan Bennett's in *For Heaven's Sake,* with Clifton Webb.

Another good offbeat role came along in 1947. This was *Nightmare Alley,* a circus story starring Tyrone Power. But good though she was, and warm and lovable, she was by now doing a parody of the earlier Blondell.

Still, she was far from finished. She was useful in *The Opposite Sex,* a generally disappointing remake of *The Women.* She was fine in *The Blue Veil,* starring Jane Wyman. And she was Katharine Hepburn's co-worker and friend in *The Desk Set,* with Spencer Tracy as the ogre who threatens to have a computer replace all those nice researchers.

The same year she had a good supporting role in *Will Success Spoil Rock Hunter,* with Tony Randall and Jayne Mansfield.

In 1965, she was fine as a New Orleans fancy lady in *The Cincinnati Kid,* with Steve McQueen and Edward G. Robinson. And two years later she was a madam in an offbeat western called *Waterhole Number Three,* with James Coburn and Carroll O'Connor.

Miss Blondell was a kind of mother hen in a TV series called called "Here Come the Brides," which was a moderate hit. And, apparently inevitably, she wound up in an Elvis Presley film, *Stay Away, Joe,* in 1968.

At sixty-four, she still had the bounce, the eyes could still light up, the smile was as bright as ever, and audiences still got a kick out of seeing her, whenever she turned up in a television special or a movie.

Those movie musicals of the 1930s and 1940s unearthed still more Bosom Buddies, some of whom achieved a respectable measure of popularity.

One of them was Martha Raye, the large-mouthed

Double or Nothing. Useful buddy Martha Raye, right, joins Bing Crosby and Mary Carlisle for a finger-snapping song. (Paramount, 1937)

broad comedienne with faultless legs and a disarming way of making her own lack of glamor work for her.

She is remembered best for her contributions to a number of Bing Crosby movies of the 1930s— *Waikiki Wedding, Double or Nothing, Rhythm on the Range*—alternating between friend of the hero and friend of the heroine. For a time, Paramount teamed her with Bob Burns, the bazooka-playing rustic, in a couple of Crosby films. They were an unusual combination—Burns shy and sly, Raye forward and foolish—but Burns's early death ended the collaboration.

Then Martha Raye became Paramount's all-around supporting comedienne—with Bob Hope in *College Swing;* with Dorothy Lamour and Ray Milland in *Tropic Holiday;* with Hope again in *Give Me a Sailor* and in *Never Say Die;* with Joe E. Brown in *One Thousand Dollars a Touchdown;* with Charlie Ruggles in *The Farmer's Daughter.*

Even after she left Paramount, it went pretty much the same way: she was teamed with Joe Penner in *The Boys from Syracuse* (Universal, 1940), and with Jack Oakie in *Navy Blues* (Warner Brothers, 1941), and Abbott and Costello in *Keep 'Em Flying* (Universal, 1941), and Olsen and Johnson in *Helzapoppin'* (also Universal, 1941).

There was a long absence then, until 1947, when Charlie Chaplin gave her a good role in his generally rejected antiwar comedy, *Monsieur Verdoux.* Later, Miss Raye found a whole new audience with her television variety shows.

At 20th Century-Fox, long-stemmed Charlotte Greenwood performed much the same function— though perhaps with a rather less explosive personality—in a series of musicals in the 1940s. Of broad shoulder and sympathetic countenance, she was a handy crying towel for Betty Grable in *Down Argentine Way* (1940), *Moon over Miami, Tall Dark and Handsome* (1941), and *Springtime in the Rockies* (1942). In 1943, it was Alice Faye whom Miss Greenwood consoled in *The Gang's All Here.* In 1944, she was with Walter Brennan and Lon McAllister in *Home in Indiana,* a little homier than usual. By 1947 it was *Wake Up and Dream,* with John Payne and June Haver, and two years later with Miss Haver and Mark Stevens in *Oh, You Beautiful Doll.*

Not until 1955, with the filming of *Oklahoma!,* did Miss Greenwood get the plum of her career:

Tall, Dark, and Handsome. Cesar Romero is turning on the charm for Virginia Gilmore. But don't worry, Charlotte Greenwood is there to guard her virtue. (20th Century-Fox, 1941)

My Sister Eileen. Janet Leigh, center, is the younger McKinney sister in this version. That's Kurt Kasznar as one of the lurking wolves, and Betty Garrett as the handy older sister. (Columbia, 1955)

88

the role of crusty, kindly Aunt Eller, friend to both hero and heroine in the Rodgers-Hammerstein musical.

Another gifted musical comedy lady who came from the stage was Betty Garrett, first starred on Broadway in *Call Me Mister,* in 1946. She was soon in Hollywood, doing double duty as friend-to-heroine and wench-to-second-male-lead. She was in *Words and Music,* a highly unlikely biography of Rodgers and Hart (Tom Drake and Mickey Rooney) in 1948. She was in *Take Me Out to the Ballgame,* with Esther Williams getting Gene Kelly and Frank Sinatra left over for Betty. She was Esther Williams's buddy in *Neptune's Daughter.* Rather more successful was *On the Town,* with Sinatra, Ann Miller, Betty Garrett, and Jules Munshin.

After Rosalind Russell became a Broadway smash hit in *Wonderful Town,* based on *My Sister Eileen,* Columbia, who owned the screen rights to the original—but not the Leonard Bernstein-Betty Comden-Adolph Green score—decided to do an "original" musical called *My Sister Eileen.* It had Janet Leigh as Eileen and Betty Garrett as the older sister. But not much else.

It was shortly after this that Miss Garrett's husband, Larry Parks, so recently hailed as the on-screen Al Jolson, ran afoul of Hollywood's me-too witch hunt and found himself persona non grata in movieland. Whether out of loyalty to him or through guilt by association, Miss Garrett's career also came to a standstill. Some eighteen years later, she turned up as Archie Bunker's new neighbor on the television series, "All in the Family."

Then there was Ann Miller, who spent a couple of decades being compared to Eleanor Powell. A skillful dancer and an attractive doll, she nevertheless somehow seemed to lack the warmth to be a successful leading lady. A bit of the Classic Bitch came through in her screen personality, even when she was being chum to some hero or heroine.

Even so, she made a good many movies, starting with *Life of the Party* (1937) with Gene Raymond and Harriet Hilliard. She was in *Stage Door* the same year, along with Katharine Hepburn and Ginger Rogers. She supported Rogers again (with Douglas Fairbanks, Jr.) in *Having Wonderful Time.* She had a good kookie role—as a mad would-be ballerina—in *You Can't Take It with You.* She was Number Two to Lucille Ball in *Too Many Girls* (1940), and to Judy Garland in *Easter Parade* (1948).

You Can't Take It with You. Ann Miller, here preoccupied with Dub Taylor, played second fiddle/friend to many a heroine. (Columbia, 1938)

Kiss Me Kate, despite its 3D gimmick, gave Ann Miller the delightful role of Bianca and she made the most of it. But then it was back to second leads in musicals: with Tony Martin and Janet Leigh in *Two Tickets to Broadway;* with Kathryn Grayson and Howard Keel in *Lovely To Look At;* with Jane Powell, Debbie Reynolds, and Tony Martin in *Hit the Deck* (1955). And then, along with virtually every other female on the MGM lot, she was in *The Opposite Sex* (*The Women*) in 1956.

Having mentioned Lucille Ball in passing, it's worth adding that long, long before she became the queen of television comedy, she had her years (up and down) in Hollywood. The "up" years are too well known to go into, but it should be noted that Miss Ball spent some years in supporting roles.

As early as 1937, for instance, she was dressing up such items as *That Girl from Paris,* with Lily Pons and Gene Raymond, and the aforementioned *Stage Door,* with Hepburn and Rogers. She supported Irene Dunne and Douglas Fairbanks, Jr., in *The Joy of Living* (1938) and even Chester Morris and Wendy Barrie in *Five Came Back.* There was a 1940 quickie called *Dance, Girl, Dance,* which starred Maureen O'Hara and Louis Hayward, and even a Charlie McCarthy-Edgar Bergen comedy in 1941 titled *Look Who's Laughing.* In 1945, she had a good supporting role in *Without Love,* with Spencer Tracy and Katharine Hepburn. Not long after that, she turned the corner on supporting roles, and soon turned her major attention to television.

Too Many Girls. Ann Miller and Desi Arnaz look great
on the dance floor, but Lucille Ball and Richard Carl-
son were the romantic leads. (RKO, 1940)

Look Who's Laughing. Lucille Ball, here reduced to feeding straight lines to Charlie McCarthy and Edgar Bergen, did her share of Bosom Buddying. (RKO, 1940)

Best Foot Forward. Nancy Walker proved a welcome friend in several musicals, including this one with Tommy Dix and Donald MacBride. (MGM, 1943)

A Girl in Every Port. You can't go much higher than trading jokes with Groucho Marx, which Marie Wilson did in this one. (RKO, 1952)

Another Broadway refugee was Nancy Walker, whose pugnacious manner was, to put it mildly, distinctive. She first supported Mickey Rooney and Judy Garland in *Girl Crazy* (1943), followed by *Best Foot Forward,* with Lucille Ball and June Allyson. Next came *Broadway Rhythm* (1944) with George Murphy and Ginny Simms.

But her appeal seemed to work better on the stage, so it was ten years before she made another movie: *Lucky Me,* with Doris Day and Robert Cummings. In 1972, she turned up as Valerie Harper's broadly Jewish mother on the "Mary Tyler Moore (TV) Show."

Hollywood's most successful dumb blonde was Marie Wilson, who started in the Warners pony stable. But in 1936 she was cast as Warren Williams's dumb secretary in *Satan Met a Lady* (that mangled version of *The Maltese Falcon*) and probably set the pattern for years of Marie Wilson roles to come. She dead-panned her way through *China Clipper* (1936) with Pat O'Brien and Beverly Roberts; *The Great Garrick* (1937), with Brian Aherne and Olivia de Havilland; *Boy Meets Girl* (1938), with James Cagney and Pat O'Brien; *Shine On Harvest Moon* (1944), with Ann Sheridan and Dennis Morgan; and numerous other routine films.

In 1949, she had the title role in *My Friend Irma,* which served to introduce to movie-goers the comedy team of Martin and Lewis. There was the inescapable sequel, *My Friend Irma Goes West,* after which the Irma character was put to use in a television series starring Miss Wilson.

Not all Bosom Buddies were comediennes, and thus far only one of the "serious" friends has been mentioned, Geraldine Fitzgerald.

Going even farther back than Miss Fitzgerald's debut, there was Margaret Lindsay, a recruit from the stage, where she picked up that knack for sounding faintly British. It served her well in such early films as *Voltaire,* with George Arliss, and *Cavalcade,* with Clive Brook and Diana Wynard (both in 1933). By 1935, she was in *Bordertown,* with Paul Muni and Bette Davis, playing a mildly bitchy society lady who toyed with Muni's affections.

In *Green Light,* a 1937 maudlin drama based on a Lloyd C. Douglas book, Errol Flynn was a surgeon, Anita Louise was the girl who blamed him for killing her mother, and Margaret Lindsay was the nice nurse who straightened out the whole mess.

The following year, Miss Lindsay was in *Jezebel,*

My Friend Irma. Marie Wilson, the perennial dumb blond, played numerous buddy roles before advancing to leads. With her here is John Lund. (Paramount, 1949)

somewhat blurred by the dazzle of Bette Davis. She was the one Henry Fonda married, after a spat with Bette, but her role was one-dimensional and colorless.

That was about as close as Margaret Lindsay got to top-drawer movies. After that came a succession of nice secretaries to lawyers, girl reporters, understanding assistants, and aides to private detectives like Ellery Queen.

One thinks, too, of Virginia Field, an attractive and able actress who never quite made it above the title. She was in *Lloyds of London,* with Tyrone Power and Madeleine Carroll, but to no avail. She was in films with both Charlie Chan (Warner Oland) and Mr. Moto (Peter Lorre), Hollywood's twin nods to Oriental wisdom.

She was with George Sanders and Dolores Del Rio in *Lancer Spy* (1937) and *Bridal Suite* (1939) with Robert Young and Annabella, and *Eternally Yours,* with Loretta Young and David Niven.

In 1940, Virginia Field got her best Bosom Buddy role in *Waterloo Bridge,* with Robert Taylor and Vivien Leigh. Miss Field it was who, when Vivien was alone and unable to make ends meet, introduced her to the oldest profession, setting off the chain reaction that included the raising of (mother) Lucille Watson's eyebrows and the bridge leap that Vivien resorted to as a solution to her problems—and the censor's.

She brings to mind June Havoc, who saw service in a number of supporting roles without ever

Jezebel. Margaret Lindsay had a good hold on Henry
Fonda, but that was before Bette Davis went to bat.
(Warner Brothers, 1938)

Waterloo Bridge. When Vivien Leigh couldn't make a
living, friend Virginia Field led her down the path
to prostitution in this drama. (MGM, 1940)

Chicago Deadline. Donna Reed played the lead, and June Havoc was in her traditional role of best friend. (Paramount, 1949)

Gentlemen's Agreement. Celeste Holm, right, was a true friend to all hands in this fine drama. With her above are the three stars, John Garfield, Gregory Peck, and Dorothy McGuire. (20th Century-Fox, 1947)

achieving stardom. She was with Rosalind Russell and Brian Aherne in the premusical (1942) version of *My Sister Eileen*. The next year it was *No Time for Love*, with Claudette Colbert and Fred Mac-Murray. In 1949, she was in *Chicago Deadline*, a newspaper yarn with Alan Ladd and Donna Reed. Earlier she appeared in *Brewster's Millions*, this particular version with Dennis O'Keefe and Helen Walker.

It was 1947's *Gentlemen's Agreement* that gave June Havoc a role worth remembering. She was the Jewish secretary encountered by Gregory Peck in his exploration of anti-Semitism—Jewish but not willing to lift a finger to help in his exposé.

Mention of *Gentlemen's Agreement* brings to mind one of the best, one of the most talented and appealing of all Hollywood's Bosom Buddies—Celeste Holm.

Another Broadway recruit (she was the original Ado Annie in *Oklahoma!*), she turned up first in *Three Little Girls in Blue*. Typically, she wasn't any of them; they were Vivian Blaine, June Haver, and Vera-Ellen.

But the next year, she was cast in *Gentlemen's Agreement*. As a witty but warm-hearted fashion editor she managed to hold her own with such stars as Gregory Peck, Dorothy McGuire, and John Garfield, and ended up winning an Oscar as best supporting actress of that year.

However satisfying that may have been, she was already doomed to Bosom Buddying. In 1948, she

was in *Road House*, with Ida Lupino and Cornel Wilde, playing a witty cashier. In 1949 it was *Come to the Stable*, with Loretta Young. They were both nuns, so nobody got any man, but Loretta was still the star. Both were nominated for Oscars, but neither won. Also in 1949, Miss Holm had a leading role, opposite Dan Dailey, in *Chicken Every Sunday*. As usual, she was convincing, but the story had a little too much chicken fat to do her career much good.

Miss Holm's third Oscar nomination came in 1950 with *All About Eve*. Here she was Bette Davis's best friend (and principal narrator of the story) who recklessly causes Miss Davis, playing a big but insecure Broadway actress, to miss a performance. Result: Anne Baxter went on in her place and proceeded to jeopardize both Bette's career and her romance.

She was Frank Sinatra's chum in *The Tender Trap* (1955). Her role was yet another variation on the Ruth McKinney part so well delineated in *My Sister Eileen*: a spinster of charm whose sharp tongue tends to scare men off. The following year, she was with Sinatra again in *High Society*, the musical remake of *The Philadelphia Story*. As Ruth Hussey had done with James Stewart in the earlier version, Celeste longed for Sinatra, but had to wait until he got over his yen for Grace Kelly.

In a dozen years, Celeste Holm left a strong enough impression that one still thinks of her as the ideal Bosom Buddy—warm, witty, accepting graciously her subordination to the glamorous star.

Only Aline MacMahon, in a much earlier era, came close to having the same sort of appeal, even though she was not as attractive physically as Miss Holm.

Aline MacMahon started her movie work in 1931, but one recalls her first in *The Mouthpiece*, in which she was the wise and friendly secretary to lawyer Warren William. She followed it with *One Way Passage*, the Kay Francis-William Powell sudser, and then *Gold Diggers of 1933*, in which she was (what else) a gold digger.

By 1935 she had worked her way up to a fine leading role in *Kind Lady*, in which she was a friendly spinster terrorized by a ruthless pauper she had befriended (Basil Rathbone).

After more inconsequential films—*When You're in Love* (1937) with Grace Moore and Cary Grant; *The Lady Is Willing* (1942) with Marlene Dietrich

Chicken Every Sunday. One of those rare occasions when Buddy types get starring roles. With Celeste Holm above is Dan Dailey. (20th Century-Fox, 1949)

Gold Diggers of 1933. Aline MacMahon, a veteran
friend, does some extra digging with Guy Kibbee in
this early musical. (Warner Brothers, 1933)

The Search. Aline MacMahon played a kindly overseas social worker in this postwar film about a dis-
placed boy. (MGM, 1948)

and Fred MacMurray—she did somewhat better in *Guest in the House* (1945) as a wary aunt in a home invaded by a trouble-making Anne Baxter. And in *The Search* (1948) she was a sympathetic, kindly UNRRA worker trying to help European refugee children.

With age, Miss MacMahon was somehow re-shaped into a likable but not especially acerbic observer of the nonsense around her, as she had been in her early Bosom Buddy days.

But this can hardly be said of the delightful Thelma Ritter, who spent many seasons on the stage before turning up in Hollywood in 1947. Her first role was in *Miracle on 34th Street,* but that bit of whimsy had too many other charms to allow her to stand out.

In *A Letter To Three Wives* (1949), however, she gave stiffer competition to the likes of Linda Darnell, Paul Douglas, Kirk Douglas, and Ann Sothern. Miss Ritter was the beer-swigging neighbor of Linda Darnell's mother (Connie Gilchrist) and managed to draw attention to herself in every scene she played. (Some other Thelma Ritter roles will be discussed in another category.)

She was equally effective in *Pickup on South Street* (1953) in which she helped Richard Widmark trap some bad guys and was killed for her trouble.

Well supplied with irreverent one-liners, she was Jane Wyman's friend in *Lucy Gallant,* Deborah Kerr's in *The Proud and the Profane,* and Joanne Woodward's in *A New Kind of Love.*

The Proud and the Profane. Thelma Ritter is at the wheel, casting a friendly glance at Deborah Kerr, who looks as if she can use a buddy. (Paramount, 1956)

Cover Girl. The title referred to Rita Hayworth, but Eve Arden, above, covered the laughs. Watching her are Lee Bowman and Otto Kruger. (Columbia, 1944)

Another enjoyable Ritter role was in *The Misfits,* as confidante to Marilyn Monroe. Sadly, Miss Ritter, like all the other principals in that John Huston-Arthur Miller film—Miss Monroe, Clark Gable, Montgomery Clift—is now dead.

If any one actress could combine the best attributes of all the most successful Bosom Buddies—Thelma Ritter's irreverence, Celeste Holm's warmth, Joan Blondell's endurance, Glenda Farrell's sarcasm, Aline MacMahon's wisdom—she would have been the greatest friend a leading lady ever had.

And she was. She was Eve Arden. (And, though less frequently seen, she still is.)

Eve Arden did it all. For two decades she was secretary, confidante, reporter, neighbor, busybody, husband-hunter, loyal friend, showgirl, gold digger, and all-around pal.

She see-sawed between ogling men with almost obscene yearning and commenting to leading ladies that all men were brutes. She was one of those actresses who leave you with the belief that she could get laughs by reading a telephone book aloud.

In *Stage Door* (1937) she was the wisest-cracking of the brittle young hopefuls who longed for theatrical careers. She was a husband hunter at a summer resort in *Having Wonderful Time* (1938). She was Harriet Hilliard's pal in *Cocoanut Grove,* the same year.

"Remember, honey," she would console a heroine who had just been mistreated by some faithless playboy, "time wounds all heels."

She was reporter Clark Gable's tough but likable colleague in *Comrade X* (1940), but it was Hedy Lamarr he loved. She was a secretary, all wise and knowing, in *That Uncertain Feeling.* She was Joan Bennett's patient roommate in *They Knew All The Answers.*

She was a wily assistant fashion editor in *Cover Girl* (1944) with Gene Kelly and Rita Hayworth. In *Mildred Pierce* (1945), seeing the heartless way Ann Blyth treated her mother (Joan Crawford), Miss Arden commented: "Alligators have the right idea—they eat their young."

She was Barbara Stanwyck's neighbor in *My Reputation* (1946) and a funny busybody in *The Voice of the Turtle* (1947). She was Joan Crawford's loyal chum again in *Goodbye My Fancy* (1951).

In *One Touch of Venus* (1948) Ava Gardner was supposed to be a Greek statue who came to life. But the only one who really came to life was Eve Arden.

Having thus spent some fifteen years honing her style and establishing a firm public image, Miss Arden took on television with a vengeance. Her series, "Our Miss Brooks," broke in as a radio show, then lasted five funny years on TV.

After that she was back in feature films, notably in *Anatomy of a Murder* (1959), in which she was country lawyer James Stewart's nagging but loyal secretary.

Complaining to Stewart that she needs a new typewriter because the "p" and the "f" don't work, she explains that she can't help typing "the arty o' the irst art."

In another scene, she says: "I was going over your check book yesterday. I can't pay me my salary."

The following year, Miss Arden was cast in the film version of William Inge's play, *The Dark at the Top of the Stairs.* Whatever merits the film may have had, it did little for Eve Arden. You kept waiting for her to drop a zinger now and then, but it was a straight role (originated by Eileen Heckart on the stage) and she was restricted to delivering the mirthless lines of a gabby, domineering wife.

Then she returned to television in still another successful series—though not as big a hit as "Our Miss Brooks." This was called "The Mothers-In-Law," with Kaye Ballard as her sidekick.

One can hope, of course, that Eve Arden will

My Reputation. George Brent and Barbara Stanwyck
starred, with John Ridgley and Eve Arden assisting.
(Warner Brothers, 1946)

One Touch of Venus. Eve Arden takes the oath for
Tom Conway in this scene. But Eve would do anything
to protect a friend. (Universal, 1950)

Anatomy of a Murder. No lawyer ever had a more entertaining secretary than Eve Arden. The lucky lawyer was James Stewart. In the middle is Arthur O'Connell. (Columbia, 1959)

come back, that Celeste Holm will again brighten screens with her sunny, oval face, that Betty Garrett will emerge again, that Joan Blondell will find a role worthy of all that exuberance.

But it doesn't seem too likely. Most of these good ladies are well past their prime now; some of them have gone from our midst.

More to the point, perhaps, the role of Bosom Buddy has pretty well outlived its usefulness. In a time when the heroine can do practically anything (right there on the screen) there's not much point in having a Bosom Buddy around to protect her against any pitfalls.

4

Old Biddies and Maiden Aunts

If Hollywood has rarely reflected life as it is, it has often reflected life as it ought to be. Thus, it seems only fair—and Hollywood helped to perpetuate the thought—that if a woman didn't have children of her own to worry about, she at least should have a niece, nephew, ward, or fortuitously acquired urchin upon whom she could impose discipline, shower affection, or bestow wealth.

Failing that, a woman of strong character (translation: postglamor years) could be useful for throwing monkey wrenches into harmless romances, spreading malicious gossip around town, viewing with alarm the new minister or teacher or doctor's wife, subsidizing the education of a promising (though sometimes perfidious) young dolt, avenging some imagined wrong done her ancestors by society, or demonstrating that a crusty exterior frequently served to camouflage a soft heart, or vice versa.

Without having experienced the pain of giving birth, the maiden aunt could feel deep affection for an orphaned niece or nephew. Without ever having had a fulfilling love affair, she could vicariously have the joy of helping young lovers. Or, if the character was more shallow, without understanding the tribulations of the heroine, she could cause no end of plot complications by gossiping or otherwise making her disapproval known.

This would seem to leave a fairly wide range of histrionic interpretation to the actresses who, for

one reason or another, spent most of their working years playing Old Biddies and Maiden Aunts.

The premiere spinster of them all was that elongated ramrod of an aunt, Edna May Oliver. With her shoehorn of a face, her stiff-backed bearing, her perpetually disapproving look, she yet managed to convey the feeling that she cared far more for her youthful charges than pride would let her admit.

Some of her performances are ineradicable. Although W. C. Fields, as Mr. Micawber, virtually stole the show in the 1935 David O. Selznick production of *David Copperfield,* Miss Oliver's Aunt Betsy was not far behind. Her agitated way of expressing both approval and disagreement made her stand out. She had a way of calling young people "Child," as if they neither had nor deserved a name, yet you knew she loved them.

She had begun to develop that style much earlier, of course. She was in silent films and in such earlier talkies as *Cimarron* (1931) with Irene Dunne and Richard Dix, and *Little Women* (1933) as the forbidding Aunt March, who was rather softer than she pretended to be.

In 1936, she was a compassionate and troubled Nurse to Norma Shearer in MGM's brave (if flawed) *Romeo and Juliet.* She suffered (as did the audience) through the clumsily plotted love affair between Clark Gable and Myrna Loy in *Parnell* (1937), and clucked sympathetically for Eleanor Powell in *Rosalie,* with Nelson Eddy. She was Sonja

David Copperfield. Young Freddie Bartholomew, in
the title role, found much warmth under Edna May
Oliver's craggy exterior. (MGM, 1935)

Romeo and Juliet. John Barrymore as Mercutio and
Edna May Oliver as Nurse, in the version starring Leslie Howard and Norma Shearer. (MGM, 1936)

Henie's Aunt Phoebe in *Second Fiddle* (1939) and filled the void left by Helen Broderick, a traditional Astaire-Rogers supporter, in *The Story of Vernon and Irene Castle.*

In 1940, she was a snooty Lady Catherine in *Pride and Prejudice,* with Greer Garson and Laurence Olivier. She had already been George Murphy's grouchy aunt in *Little Miss Broadway,* a Shirley Temple opus, and remarkably poised in *Drums Along the Mohawk,* with Claudette Colbert.

Dead more than thirty years now, Edna May Oliver remains vividly alive in her screen image, not merely because she is still available on the late television shows but because she had such a distinctive style and a commanding personality.

Not quite her equal but also effective was the late Helen Westley, the resident Old Biddy at 20th Century-Fox, as Miss Oliver was at MGM.

Her early films included *Death Takes a Holiday, The House of Rothschild,* and *Anne of Green Gables,* all in 1934. Two years later, she was the stern but lovable Parthy in *Showboat,* watching Magnolia (Irene Dunne) fall in love with the riverboat gambler Gaylord Ravenal (Allan Jones) and unable to stop it.

Next came a string of Shirley Temple films: *Dimples* and *Stowaway* (both in 1936), *Heidi* (1937), and *Rebecca of Sunnybrook Farm* (1938). To some degree or other, in all of these she was alternately crochety and sentimental, almost a jowly imitation of Edna May Oliver, yet with a commanding presence of her own.

Her career as pseudogrouch went on. She was Aunt Sophie in *Alexander's Ragtime Band* (1938) and Grandma Leonard in *Lillian Russell* (1940). In between, she consoled but didn't hesitate to

Anne of Green Gables. Anne Shirley, all innocence, is confronted by a stern Helen Westley in this sentimental story. (RKO, 1934)

Heidi. Shirley Temple snuggled comfortably in the embrace of a mellower Helen Westley. (20th Century-Fox, 1937)

scold Claudette Colbert in *Zaza* (1939), Ingrid Bergman in *Adam Had Four Sons* (1941), and Loretta Young in *Bedtime Story* (1941).

Like Miss Oliver, she died in 1942 (she was four years older) and also like Miss Oliver she is remembered with affection by movie buffs of that era.

Still more transparently grumpy was the marvelous May Robson, who, coincidentally, died in the same year. Born the year the Civil War ended, she was in silent films from 1915.

She was already sixty-eight when she was starred in *Lady for a Day,* based on the Damon Runyon fable about Apple Annie, and she was a heartwarming old rummy. That was in 1933.

The same year she was playboy Franchot Tone's deaf but salty grandmother in *Dancing Lady,* with Joan Crawford. She was Clark Gable's mischievous mother in *Wife Versus Secretary* (1936) and Errol Flynn's autocratic aunt in *The Perfect Specimen* (1937).

Also in 1937, she was the kindly grandmother of Esther Victoria Blodgett, who gave the stage-

struck young girl the money to go to Hollywood and become Vicki Lester in *A Star Is Born.* (The girl was Janet Gaynor).

Miss Robson was imperious in *Bringing Up Baby* (1938) with Cary Grant and Katharine Hepburn. And she was the perfect Aunt Polly in *The Adventures of Tom Sawyer,* the same year.

But she won even more hearts that year in *Four Daughters* as the aunt of Priscilla, Rosemary, and Lola Lane and Gale Page, smacking snoopy hands with a wooden spoon, nagging at Claude Rains (the girls' father) and revelling in the outrageous flatterings of Jeffrey Lynn and John Garfield.

She grumped and growled and glowed her way through three more films in that mawkish series: *Daughters Courageous* and *Four Wives* (1939) and *Four Mothers* (1941), all with much the same cast.

Not as well known by name, but with a familiar face, Florence Bates devoted much of her film career to playing unpleasant Old Biddies who had no heart to hide. Most of her characterizations were broad, so that she was useful in comedies that called for older Classic Bitches.

A one-time lawyer who turned to acting in middle life, she was fifty when she made her first movie, but it turned out to be a big one: *Rebecca.* Miss Bates played an insufferable dowager, rude to the help and totally detestable.

In *Kitty Foyle* (1941) she looked scornfully down her Philadelphia nose at Ginger Rogers. In *The Devil and Miss Jones,* she was mean to poor Spring Byington. In *Saratoga Trunk* (1945) with Gary Cooper and Ingrid Bergman, she was an ogre named Mrs. Coventry Bellop.

The Secret Life of Walter Mitty (1947), the Danny Kaye version of the James Thurber classic, gave her the role of a terrifyingly domineering mother-in-law and she played it magnificently.

One of her choicest cameos was in *A Letter to Three Wives,* the witty Joseph L. Mankiewicz film of 1949. Ann Sothern was a soap-opera writer (married to Kirk Douglas) forced to kow-tow to her sponsor and, more importantly, to his wife. Hobart Cavanaugh, an appropriately sheepish actor, was the sponsor and the arch ogre, Florence Bates, was his smug wife.

Somewhat similar in build—plump and matronly —but far different in personality was Alison Skipworth, who played haughty wealthy ladies at times.

Four Mothers. White-haired May Robson was the kindliest of old biddies. From left above are Dick Foran, Miss Robson, Lola Lane, Eddie Albert, Gale Page, Rosemary Lane, and Priscilla Lane. (Warner Brothers, 1941)

On the Town. Florence Bates, a grouchy old biddy, stares down Gene Kelly. At left is Frank Sinatra. (MGM, 1949)

If I Had a Million. Alison Skipworth, left, and Cecil Cunningham. Miss Skipworth was paired with W. C. Fields in this lively comedy. (Paramount, 1932)

Andy Hardy's Blonde Trouble. Whatever troubles Andy had, he had a nice, warm family, including Ma (Fay Holden) and Pa (Lewis Stone), plus Sara Haden, center, as the resident maiden aunt. (MGM, 1944)

But her dowagers were so obviously fraudulent that one was delighted by them. She was equally adept at playing amusing low-brows.

Many late show fans have probably seen her (possibly without knowing her name) in a memorable sequence in *If I Had a Million* (1932), in which she and W. C. Fields took their sudden wealth as a signal to drive around town in their old jalopy smashing into an endless procession of road hogs.

Two years before that she was in *Outward Bound,* that spooky play about a shipload of people who are dead but don't know it. Miss Skipworth was "Mrs. Clivedon-Banks," and she played the role as if the hyphen were a medal she had earned.

Fine though she was in such roles, Miss Skipworth seemed even more at home playing down-at-heels women who still had enough gumption left to put up a front. In *The Girl from Tenth Avenue* (1935) she was Bette Davis's landlady, an ex-Floradora girl who undertakes to give Bette a touch of class.

In *Dangerous* (also 1935) she was the caretaker at Franchot Tone's country home, who views with disapproval Bette Davis's insistence upon drinking. A year later, she was in *The Princess Comes Across,* with Carole Lombard and Fred MacMurray. Carole was a phony princess and Miss Skipworth was her equally fraudulent ally.

Then came *Satan Met a Lady,* a 1936 turkey that almost deserves a chapter by itself, if only to show how badly a good story can be mangled. The story in this case was Dashiell Hammett's classic, *The Maltese Falcon.* (It was first made, with its original title, in 1931 with Ricardo Cortez and Bebe Daniels.) Warren William played Ted Shayne (changed from Sam Spade) and Bette Davis was the sultry temptress who tried to lead him astray. But the wildest idea of all was changing Gutman (Dudley Digges in the 1931 version, Sydney Greenstreet in 1941) into a woman, renaming her Madame Barabbas, and casting Alison Skipworth in the part.

She was in movies for only three more years (although she lived until 1952) but one wonders how seriously she could have taken any role after Madame Barabbas.

Another busy Old Biddy and/or Maiden Aunt was Sara Haden, but hers was a schizophrenic

Night Must Fall. Dame May Whitty was such an irritating old biddy that Robert Montgomery might have been justified in wanting to do her in. (MGM, 1937)

screen existence. A stiff-backed, prim-looking woman, she was adept at playing smalltown gossips, disapproving neighbors, unemotional aides to ruthless bankers, starchy head nurses.

She could be heartless to Shirley Temple, in *Captain January* and *Poor Little Rich Girl,* and in between be mean to Jane Withers in *Little Miss Nobody,* all in 1936.

But there was another side to Sara Haden, a warmer, more bending side. She was a familiar fixture in the Hardy home, playing the always-on-hand, usually understanding, occasionally baffled maiden aunt. In that role, she appeared in all but two of the sixteen Hardy family movies, between 1937 and 1958. And that last one (*Andy Hardy Comes Home*) was also Sara Haden's last movie.

Then there was Dame May Whitty, a formidable old biddy who graced some twenty-eight films in the dozen years she spent on the screen—starting at the age of seventy-two.

Her first was probably her best: *Night Must Fall,* with Robert Montgomery as the psychopathic killer who plots Dame May's demise. The old lady, selfish tyrant confined to a wheelchair, is enchanted by the glib, flattering Danny, who insinuates himself into her household and becomes her favorite. One almost wanted to see Danny's plot succeed.

Dame May was more likable in the Alfred Hitchcock thriller, *The Lady Vanishes,* in which she played the title role: Miss Froy, a gabby old traveler whose disappearance triggers one of Hitchcock's most fascinating tales.

In 1940, she was Aunt Hester in a pallid remake of *A Bill Of Divorcement,* with Maureen O'Hara and Adolph Menjou attempting the roles played earlier (and so much better) by Katharine Hepburn and John Barrymore.

In *Mrs. Miniver* (1942) she was Lady Beldon, a symbol of the pride and grace of the British aristocracy in the face of Hitler's expected invasion.

And the following year, she was Greer Garson's mother-in-law in *Madame Curie,* not a particularly meaty role for one of her abilities, but acceptable nevertheless.

Unquestionably, the most successful Old Biddy of them all—even before she was old—was Zasu Pitts. Her unsteady voice and twittering hands became so familiar that no mimic or impressionist could resist "doing" her. And if that seems a small thing, stop to consider whether you have ever seen anybody do an impression of Edna May Oliver or, for that matter, Joan Fontaine. It's the distinctive ones, the Cagneys, Bogarts, Davises, Hepburns, and Gables that can be more convincingly caricatured. And Zasu Pitts.

In her forty years in Hollywood, this remarkable actress appeared in more than one hundred films, the first twenty or so silents. Perhaps even

Thirteen Hours by Air. The little monster above was in the care of Zasu Pitts, right, who looks appropriately dismayed. (Paramount, 1936)

more remarkably, a clear majority of them were B pictures. Yet, so individual was her personality, so strong her public image, that she became a kind of "star," if not in the sense that people went out of their way to see her films, at least to the extent that she was as familiar to audiences as a member of the family, much as television "characters" were to become to a later generation.

She was, however briefly, in *The Little Princess,* in 1917, but someone named Mary Pickford was the center of attention. By 1919, in *Better Times,* she was beginning to take on that vulnerable look that was to serve her so well for decades to come. In 1922, she was in *Is Matrimony a Failure,* which may have inadvertently hinted at her future screen career—four decades of spinsterhood. The following year, she starred in Erich von Stroheim's *Greed,* looking very Lillian Gish-ish. That fragile

quality carried her through the rest of the silent era and into talkies.

After a series of ho-hum roles, she was assigned the part of Miss Hazy in *Mrs. Wiggs of the Cabbage Patch* (1934) starring Pauline Lord. This was a sentimental, hokey "family picture," saved for many by the comic fluttering of Miss Pitts and the late appearance of W. C. Fields as an anxious suitor.

Meanwhile, Zasu had already begun to build a following in B pictures, due partly to a series of flimsy comedies in which she was paired with Slim Summerville, himself a comic ugly duckling. They made five of these quickies in a row: *They Just Had To Get Married, Out All Night, Her First Mate, Love, Honor and Oh, Baby!* and *Their Big Moment.* How could anyone living in, say, rural Kansas resist going to see Zasu Pitts and Slim Sum-

Eternally Yours. David Niven toasts Virginia Field, while Zasu Pitts assumes a typically spinsterish look. (United Artists, 1939)

merville in something as provocatively titled as *They Just Had To Get Married?*

In 1935, she was in *Ruggles of Red Gap,* but surrounded by Charles Laughton, Charles Ruggles, and Mary Boland, she didn't have much chance to shine. The next year, in *Thirteen Hours by Air* (Joan Bennett and Fred MacMurray) she was good as the squeamish, airsick governess to a ten-year-old brat.

In 1937, she was one of two prissy socialite sisters (Dorothy Peterson was the other) in *Fifty Second Street,* an inept effort at exploiting the then current interest in that "swing street." In 1939, it was *Eternally Yours* (Loretta Young and David Niven) in which Zasu was the gullible wife of tycoon Raymond Walburn. In 1942, she, Marjorie Main, and Aline MacMahon were a trio of spinsters playing cupid in a bit of nonsense titled *Tish.*

And so it went, through 1950, which saw her as a fussy nurse in a psychiatric ward in *Francis,* the film in which Donald O'Connor first played second banana to a talking (voice by Chill Wills) mule.

Zasu Pitts continued for more than another decade, through *Let's Face It* (1943) with Bob Hope and Betty Hutton, and *Life With Father* (1947), in which she was useful as Cousin Cora, and another Francis picture in 1945, and a Doris Day comedy, *The Thrill of It All,* in 1963.

Her last movie, that same year, was Stanley

The Rage of Paris. Danielle Darrieux, a picture of ennui, ignores Mischa Auer's invitation, while Helen Broderick looks apprehensive. (Universal, 1938)

Kramer's crammed-full-of-comics *It's a Mad, Mad, Mad, Mad World,* in which she was lost in a platoon that included Milton Berle, Mickey Rooney, Dick Shawn, Ethel Merman, Phil Silvers, Jonathan Winters, Jimmy Durante, Ben Blue, Don Knotts, Buddy Hackett, Sid Caesar, Terry-Thomas, Buster Keaton, and just about every other comedian who wasn't otherwise employed. Playing a telephone operator, Zasu Pitts might as well have phoned it in.

Despite a career with few high spots, Zasu Pitts was somehow outstanding, as distinctive in her way as Gable or Harlow, as familiar to many millions as any president, as welcome as a delicate breeze.

Having covered most of the memorable Old Biddies and Maiden Aunts, it still remains to touch on, however briefly, a few more who should not be passed over.

Let it be noted, first of all, that Billie Burke and Spring Byington, already covered at some length in the chapter on mothers, sometimes spilled over into the category to which this section is devoted.

Once again, fleeting images haunt the mind, memories of an actress who, here and there, now and then, captured our attention as biddies or aunts:

Helen Broderick, for instance, in such early Astaire-Rogers musicals as *Top Hat* (1935) and *Swing Time* (1936).

Cora Witherspoon, that gawky treeful of birds, chirping her senseless way through *Libelled Lady* (1937), *Dark Victory,* and *The Women* (1939).

Minnie Dupree, as the proposed victim of that

Theodora Goes Wild. In the center of the shocked trio at left is Spring Byington. At right are Irene Dunne and Melvyn Douglas. (Columbia, 1936)

On the Avenue. Cora Witherspoon, at left, looked down her nose in numerous comedies. The other lady above is Madeleine Carroll, and in the center is Alan Mowbray. (20th Century-Fox, 1937)

Laura Hope Crews. As Aunt Pitty-Pat in *Gone with the Wind.* Miss Crews seemed to have been born with a hanky handy.

Kitty. Constance Collier, right, lent her considerable presence to many a film. With her above is Cecil Kellaway. The stars were Paulette Goddard and Ray Milland. (Paramount, 1945)

Patricia Collinge. A fine character actress who specialized in soft-centered aunts, mothers, and fragile old biddies.

Intruder in the Dust. Elizabeth Patterson was a proud old gal in this drama. Also above are David Brian and Claude Jarman, Jr. (MGM, 1949)

I Remember Mama. Ellen Corby, right, was a likable but flighty aunt in this family yarn. Also in the scene are Barbara Bel Geddes and Philip Dorn. (RKO, 1948)

Harvey. James Stewart can see his six-foot rabbit, and Josephine Hull thinks she can. But Charles Drake and Peggy Dow clearly can't. (Universal, 1950)

114

quartet of rogues (Roland Young, Billie Burke, Janet Gaynor, and Douglas Fairbanks, Jr.) in *The Young in Heart* (1938).

Laura Hope Crews, that indomitable mother of earlier years, as Aunt Pitty-Pat in *Gone With the Wind* (1939).

Constance Collier, that forbidding figure in *Stage Door* (1937) and *Damsel in Distress,* the same year.

Fay Bainter as Robert Young's meddling sister in *The Shining Hour* (1938).

Aline MacMahon, an appealing maiden aunt in Eugene O'Neill's *Ah, Wilderness,* back in 1935.

Patricia Collinge, so pathetic, so fragile, as one of the few likable characters in that family of wretches in *The Little Foxes* (1941).

Elizabeth Patterson, as Patricia Neal's snooty, cold aunt in *Bright Leaf* (1950).

Ellen Corby ("discovered" by television's "The Waltons" in the 1970s) as a twittering old aunt

in *I Remember Mama* (1948).

Miriam Hopkins playing Olivia de Havilland's unyielding aunt in *The Heiress* (1949).

Josephine Hull, irresistably pixilated in *Arsenic and Old Lace* (1944) and just as lovable in *Harvey* (1950).

Martita Hunt, appealingly mad as Miss Havisham in *Great Expectations* (1947).

Ethel Barrymore, commanding even in the watered-down remake of *Four Daughters,* titled *Young at Heart* (1954).

Rosalind Russell, pitiable and unpleasant as the old maid school teacher in *Picnic* (1956).

Hermione Gingold, as subtle as a pneumatic drill in *Gigi* (1958).

And Helen Hayes, arch and winsome as a professional stowaway in *Airport* (1970).

Were they all still around, they could fill a senior citizen's home and keep the place buzzing with the dazzling array of their combined thespian gifts.

Young at Heart. After the rewriting, Ethel Barrymore was the best thing left in this version of *Four Daughters.* The stars were Doris Day and Frank Sinatra. (Warner Brothers, 1954)

Picnic. Rosalind Russell was an effective spinster in the film of William Inge's play. Kim Novak is at left, Betty Field at right. (Columbia, 1956)

Airport. Likable busybody Helen Hayes helped trap the mad bomber (Van Heflin, right) in this slickly made thriller. (Universal, 1970)

Gigi. Hermione Gingold and Maurice Chevalier still enjoyed flirting with each other in this Lerner-Loewe musical. (MGM, 1958)

5

Harlots and Hookers, Hearts of Gold

Whatever literary genius invented the scarlet woman with the heart of gold—and this is no place to dwell on his identity—must have had considerable insight into the tastes, prejudices, and mores of the mass audience. The movie audience, surely indicative of mass taste, has always been a sucker for the superficially hard hooker, with soft center to be revealed upon closer scrutiny.

For a male chauvinist society, we have shown remarkable compassion for the woman on film who, for whatever bizarre combination of seedy circumstances, must turn to renting out her body to a succession of usually unsavory customers.

As for the women in our pre-Women's Lib society, they most likely harbored some deep-rooted resentment of man and found it that much easier to sympathize with a Fallen Woman, so clearly a victim of the perfidy of man.

When you come right down to it, both men and women seem to have been capable of finding it in their hearts to forgive (or, at least, refrain from condemning) the film floozies whose travails were often so movingly portrayed.

And even when a hooker wasn't all heart, we the audience could find it in our hearts to be understanding, perhaps with the magnanimity that royalty displays toward the less belligerent representatives of the bread-stealing masses.

For actresses, such roles were often tempting,

for here was a sure way to display one's courage (by playing impure characters) while also trapping an audience into sympathetic emotional involvement.

Of all the actresses who have, at one time or another, succumbed to the temptation, surely one of the most successful was Claire Trevor, who became a past mistress at the art of playing fallen women.

There was a catch in her voice that touched the heart, a look of defeat, of having been kicked around by life, that lent authenticity to her interpretations of women past redemption.

Claire Trevor had been in more than a dozen movies (starting in 1933) before she had the first of those roles which were to bring out the best in her.

This was Dead End, a stark sociological study of the ghetto (we called them slums in those days) as breeding ground of criminals. It is remembered now mostly for introducing the group of young actors who were to become known as "the Dead End Kids" (Billy Halop, Huntz Hall, Bobby Jordan, Leo Gorcey, Gabriel Dell, and, always good for a movie buff's bar bet, Bernard Punsley), but in 1937, freshly adapted from Sidney Kingsley's hit play, it was a gripping drama, skillfully directed by William Wyler and well acted by all concerned.

Humphrey Bogart was Baby Face Martin, a grad-

117

Boom Town. In westerns, like this one, hookers were usually referred to as "saloon girls." Two veteran film saloon girls are shown here: Marion Martin and Minna Gombell. The potential customers are Clark Gable and Spencer Tracy. (MGM, 1940)

ute of this East Side sewer, who returns to his old haunts to visit his mother (Marjorie Main) and his childhood sweetheart, Francey, played with stunning honesty by Claire Trevor.

When Bogart realizes that she has become the neighborhood streetwalker (while he has become a "successful" gangster) he is repulsed and demands of her: "Why didn't you starve first?"

With suitable Camille-like coughing, Miss Trevor throws the challenge back at him: "Why didn't you?"

In that moment, Miss Trevor won an Oscar nomination—and the heart of every compassionate movie goer in America. She also won a kind of label. One can visualize cigar-chewing producers plan-

ning upcoming movies: "And for the prostie, we'll get Claire Trevor."

It wasn't all like that. She also played friends to stars (Loretta Young in *Second Honeymoon*) and leading ladies in B pictures. But, somehow, she had found her profession within her profession.

If proof were needed, it came in 1939 with *Stagecoach,* now regarded as one of John Ford's masterpieces. Besides Miss Trevor, the cast included John Wayne, Thomas Mitchell, John Carradine, and Donald Meek.

Dudley Nichols wrote the screenplay, but it's difficult to resist the thought that he'd studied Guy De Maupassant's "Boule de Suif" beforehand. In that wry French tale, a scorned prostitute in the

118

Stagecoach. Claire Trevor is stared down by all the "nice" women in this early scene from the John Ford classic. But she proved to be superior to all of them. (United Artists, 1939)

1870 Franco-Prussian War is encouraged by those who look down on her to give herself to an infatuated German officer in order to save themselves. This was pretty much what Claire Trevor had to do in *Stagecoach*—except that the American west had replaced France as the setting. Once again, she was magnificent—demonstrating that the character had more courage than the "respectable" people who snubbed her—and winning for Miss Trevor her second best supporting actress nomination in three years. But still no Oscar.

Thus went Claire Trevor's career. When she wasn't going to bed (off camera) with men, she was a saloon girl (*Valley of the Giants,* 1938) or a gangster's moll (*The Amazing Dr. Clitterhouse,* 1938) or Lana Turner's hard-as-nails rival for Clark Gable (*Honky Tonk,* 1941) or the western dancehall girl loved by Bat Masterson (*Woman of the Town,* 1943) or a sluttish villainess who can hardly keep her hands off Dick Powell (*Murder, My Sweet,* 1945).

In 1948 she was Edward G. Robinson's alcoholic, defeated mistress in *Key Largo,* finally winning that Oscar that had eluded her twice before.

However handsome Oscars may look on one's mantel, they have a way of not magically changing one's career. She was William Bendix's wife in *The Babe Ruth Story* (1948) and Broderick Crawford's wife in *Stop, You're Killing Me* (1952), the latter a heavy-handed remake of the

delightful *A Slight Case of Murder.* Then it was back to loose but deep-down-decent women (*The High and the Mighty,* 1954) and saloon keepers (*Lucy Gallant,* 1955). Respectability and motherhood came in *Marjorie Morningstar* (1958). But Claire Trevor was not again to reach the heights (or the depths) of her earlier roles.

The Hollywood harlot, with or without heart of gold, neither started nor ended with Claire Trevor. Some of our finest actresses have yielded to the temptation to portray women of varying degrees of flexible morality.

Even though the primary purpose of this survey is to salute Hollywood's Other Women—the women who did not get their men, or who made most of their films in support of stars—it may be useful to include here and there some examples of stars in harlot roles, if only to indicate the various approaches to such roles.

One remembers, for example, Bette Davis in *Of Human Bondage* (1934) as Mildred, the heartless trollop who makes life hell for medical student Leslie Howard and eventually dies of whatever euphemism the movie censors of the time could find to suggest retribution.

Even before that, there was the matchless Greta Garbo, whose brilliance as a true star has not dimmed despite more than thirty years of absence from films.

Although she didn't restrict her work to fallen women, Garbo played her share of them. Well be-

Honky Tonk. Lana Turner was the nice girl here and Claire Trevor was the saloon girl. The main dish is Clark Gable. (MGM, 1941)

Flesh and the Devil. Neither John Gilbert nor audiences could resist Greta Garbo in this early romance. (MGM, 1927)

fore billboards announced to the world, in 1930, that "Garbo Talks!," she had played a vamp in *The Torrent* (1926), a hostess turned hooker in *The Temptress* (1926), and a woman of abandon in *Flesh and the Devil* (1927).

The first Garbo talking picture was *Anna Christie,* from the pen of Eugene O'Neill. Again she was a beaten prostitute seeking refuge. Her past was equally tarnished in *Inspiration* (1931) with Robert Montgomery; and *Susan Lenox: Her Fall and Rise* (1931) with Clark Gable.

Garbo kept having tragic love affairs in her next few films, though money didn't always change hands. Then came *Camille,* in 1936, considered by many Garbo buffs to be her greatest movie. She was Marguerite, a gay, happy courtesan until she falls for boyish Robert Taylor. But his father (Lionel Barrymore) persuades her to give him up, a sacrifice she makes with that nobility of character reserved for fictional ladies of the evening.

One of Joan Crawford's most successful roles in the 1930s was as Sadie Thompson in the Somerset Maugham story, *Rain* (1932). She was the island prostitute who led the Reverend Mr. Davidson (Walter Huston) astray just when he was trying to save her soul.

There have been many more instances of stars playing scarlet women, of course, but these few seem to stand out, perhaps because in the context of their time they seem relatively daring.

Moviegoers of today may seem puzzled by this, but it is necessary to see such roles as Mildred, Camille, and Sadie Thompson in their proper perspective, as regards their being portrayed on film in Hollywood movies of the 1920s and 1930s.

Camille. Marguerite, that classic courtesan, loses her heart to Armand. Greta Garbo and Robert Taylor. (MGM, 1936)

Rain. Preacher Walter Huston didn't stand a chance once he got close to Joan Crawford, as Sadie Thompson. (United Artists, 1932)

It was a time, one must strain to realize, when the impact of the movies was truly being comprehended, when pressure groups of formidable influence were being willing sentinels, protecting the "morals" of the nation, when studio heads were loath to offend any such groups, when, if you will, euphemism was in flower.

In these days, when what is being debated is how old one should be before being exposed to the graphic sexuality of *Deep Throat* or *The Devil in Miss Jones,* it must seem terribly quaint —yet it is a fact—that forty years ago the cinema was straining to stay within the bounds of a lexicon of euphemisms that included such namby-pamby sugar coatings as lady of the evening, fallen woman, woman of easy virtue, woman of the town, demi-mondaine, and erring sister, not to mention such pungent if inelegant blush-dodgers as strumpet, trollop, tart, chippy, harlot, and the borderline broad.

The film fiction of the time made other restrictions, too: if a woman must be shown to be a prostitute (and "shown" was hardly the case) it would help if it were strongly implied that she was driven to it by a heartless man, a mean stepmother, or, in a pinch, desperate social conditions. And by no means was she to enjoy her way of life: one way or another she had to pay for her sins of the flesh. Death was the best currency to square off this debt, but on occasion rehabilitation might be deemed to work.

All of this may be helpful in evaluating the popularity of a couple of typical films of the 1930s, both starring Gladys George, who had somewhat the same tarnished appeal that Claire Trevor conveyed.

Miss George had made a couple of forays into movies in the silent days, only to beat a hasty retreat to her natural habitat, the live theater. But by 1936 she was back in Hollywood, starring in *Valiant Is the Word for Carrie,* a popular novel for some years by then. As cleaned up for the movie, Carrie was a shady lady who lived on the edge of town, making her living you know how. But she turns noble when she is befriended by a small boy. The film then goes on to detail her later travails. In other words, some two thirds of the film sought to prove that her earlier "sins"—never shown on screen, of course—were being wiped off the slate.

The picture was a moderate success and was followed the next year by another standard tearjerker: the fourth movie version of *Madame X.* Probably the most daring thing in the movie was the title, if one wanted to bother remembering that a madam could conceivably have some smutty interpretation. This squeaky-clean *Madame X* had left her husband and become the mistress of a low-life gambler. When said low-life threatened to expose her and thus disgrace her son, Madame X shot him dead. And by one of those ironies loosely regarded as poetic license her own son —who, of course, doesn't know she's his mother —ends up defending her in court.

Oh, the women cried their eyes out again and the movie did reasonably well. (It was done yet one more time in 1966, with Lana Turner as the long-suffering Madame X.) It also helped to type Gladys George as a—here we go again—woman of easy virtue, usually with heart of gold.

In 1939, in *The Roaring Twenties,* she was Panama Smith (a vague take-off on Texas Guinan), a brassy speakeasy operator who befriends under-

Madame X. Giving a potential customer the once-over. The mysterious lady is Gladys George, and the man is Paul Porcasi. (MGM, 1937)

122

worldling James Cagney and sticks with him even when he hits the skids. *The Maltese Falcon* (1941) gave her a good, if small, role as the widow of Humphrey Bogart's partner, all too willing to be consoled by Bogie before her husband's body is barely cold.

In *Lady from Cheyenne* (1941) she was a saloon girl, which was the Western's euphemism for the bad guy's mistress. And in *Christmas Holiday* (1944) she was one of the distractions that kept Gene Kelly from being the husband Deanna Durbin thought he should be. In *Flamingo Road* (1949) she was the madam in a Southern brothel; and the following year, in *Bright Leaf,* she was madam Lauren Bacall's chum.

She had been tossed (back in 1938) into *Marie Antoinette,* after her initial screen success in *Valiant Is the Word for Carrie.* This costume drama had Norma Shearer in the title role, and Miss George, suitably powdered and peruked, appeared as Madame DuBarry. But evidently acting under an assumed mane wasn't Gladys's bag.

Another actress of the 1930s who managed to get into a kind of seedy rut was Isabel Jewell. She had the added advantage (or disadvantage) of looking rather run-down, thus fitting even more comfortably the stereotype of the fallen woman who pays with her health.

At any rate, she is probably best remembered in just such a role in *Lost Horizon* (1937). She

Moontide. Jean Gabin saved Ida Lupino's shattered life and, in time, love blossomed. (20th Century-Fox, 1942)

was Gloria, the doxie with the pathetic cough (shades of Camille) who is befriended by Thomas Mitchell, playing an outspoken tycoon who is a fugitive from justice. One may not regard befriending a hooker when you're trapped in Tibet as an especially humanitarian action, but that may be irrelevant.

Miss Jewell was also one of the girls in a 1937 Bette Davis film, *Marked Woman.* "One of the girls" was also a way of evading the unpleasant facts: the girls worked for a racketeer who insisted his girls cajole the customers into buying drinks. One was left to suspect that the girls hustled something more than highballs, but in 1937 the movies didn't get too explicit about that sort of thing.

Isabel Jewell was of similarly dubious virtue in a 1939 melodrama called *Missing Daughters,* with Richard Arlen and Rochelle Hudson as the leads.

About the same time Miss Jewell was coughing her way into B pictures, another slender young actress was getting more serious attention after half a dozen years of acting in Hollywood movies.

She was Ida Lupino, and in a handful of movies within a few years, she was to become established as a capable actress—but also typed as a less-than-pure woman on the screen.

Her first important role was in *The Light that Failed* (1939), a somewhat distorted version of the Kipling story about an artist going blind. Miss Lupino was a chippy Ronald Colman picked off

Lost Horizon. Among the refugees in Shangri-La was Isabel Jewell as an ailing prostitute. With her are Edward Everett Horton, John Howard, and Thomas Mitchell. (Columbia, 1937)

the streets to work as his model, too coarse and insensitive to appreciate his torment.

She was impressive enough that the following year she had a strong and even more unsympathetic role in *They Drive by Night*, starring George Raft and Ann Sheridan. This time she was married to a bore (Alan Hale) but had the yens for Raft. So she bumped off hubby and threw herself at Raft, who had better things (such as Miss Sheridan) on his mind.

Miss Lupino was more sympathetic—though not exactly virginal—in a fine 1941 melodrama, *High Sierra*, with Bogart as her leading man. She was a "dancehall girl" initially attached to hood Alan Curtis, but she soon switched allegiance to Bogie and stayed with him to the bullet-riddled finish.

In *Moontide* (1942) she was a dockside doxie on the verge of suicide when she was rescued by French star Jean Gabin (who had earlier made a better version of the story, titled *Port of Shadows*) and rehabilitated by love.

Undoubtedly sheer boredom with playing Goodie-Two-Shoes parts led many an actress to taking on films about women of less than perfect morality. This was certainly true of Bette Davis, who staged numerous rebellions (not always successfully) against studio-imposed piety. Also, some actresses were bright enough to realize they could attract more attention and prove their talent in roles with some guts to them, which frequently meant mean, selfish, slatternly, or immoral women.

Take Anne Baxter. After several years of colorless supporting roles, she had worked her way (by 1944) up to playing the nice, wholesome girls that servicemen presumably wanted to come home to: *The Sullivans, The Eve of St. Mark, Sunday Dinner for a Soldier*. Then came *Guest in the House* (1944), in which she played a scheming homewrecker, and even though her performance was widely regarded as too broad, the film opened up new vistas for her.

Soon came the role of Sophie in *The Razor's Edge* (1946), in which she went from nice Chicago girl to tragic widow to Parisian slut. And that led to Miss Baxter's Oscar as best supporting actress of the year.

Four years and several minor films later, she landed the title role in *All About Eve*, Joseph L. Mankiewicz's brilliant look backstage in the New York theater. Miss Baxter was the scheming Eve who set out to displace Bette Davis and to steal

her man (Gary Merrill). She got another Oscar nomination, as did Miss Davis, but both were nosed out by Judy Holliday—playing a dumb doxie.

The Baxter career continued its ups and downs. In *One Desire* (1955) she was a girl from the wrong side of the tracks trying to become socially acceptable. In *Three Violent Men* (1957) she was a reformed tart who became a model wife. In *Season of Passion* (1959, from the play *Summer of the Seventeenth Doll*) she was quite frankly a whore. In a generally inferior remake of *Cimarron* (1960) she was Dixie, a saloon girl. And in *Fool's Parade* (1971) she was Cleo, a riverboat madam whose establishment is visited by some escaped convicts.

Season of Passion involved two hookers who spend their summers with John Mills and Ernest Borgnine. Anne Baxter was one; the other was Angela Lansbury, one of England's most gifted exports, who toiled for two decades before achieving stardom. During those years, she played some interestingly seamy women.

In her first film, *Gaslight* (1944), she was the delicious looking maid who had eyes for Charles Boyer, the suave gentleman intent on driving his wife (Ingrid Bergman) bananas. The next year, Miss Lansbury was a saloon singer with whom Hurd Hatfield trifled in *The Picture of Dorian Gray*. In *The Harvey Girls* (1946) Miss Lansbury was in command of the honky-tonk women who tried to drive Judy Garland and her fellow waitresses out of town. And in 1947, she was a courtesan in *The Affairs of Bel Ami*.

In *The Long Hot Summer* (1958) she was Orson Welles's golden-hearted mistress. The year after that, she romped through *Season of Passion*. And in 1960, she was the widow beautician wrongly suspected of carrying on with Robert Preston in *The Dark at the Top of the Stairs*. In *Mister Buddwing* (1966) she was an open-hearted slattern who came to the aid of amnesia victim James Garner.

(Miss Lansbury's career included, of course, a wide range of roles, some of which are touched on in other sections of this book.)

The American contemporary of Miss Lansbury's who has probably put in the most time playing women-who-went-wrong-for-various-defensible-reasons is Shelley Winters.

After a number of small parts, she first at-

Season of Passion. Hooker Anne Baxter and boy friend Ernest Borgnine have finally gotten on each other's nerves, after seventeen summers. (United Artists, 1959)

tracted attention in *A Double Life,* Ronald Colman's 1948 excursion into schizophrenia. He was an actor playing Othello and getting his on-stage and off-stage emotions all fouled up. Miss Winters was his table-waiting mistress and wound up being killed by Colman.

She was still more pathetic in *A Place in the Sun,* the 1951 George Stevens rendering of Dreiser's *An American Tragedy.* Miss Winters was the not-too-bright girl who looks fine to ambitious Montgomery Clift until he spots socialite Elizabeth Taylor. Then, having switched his affection to the latter, he found himself drowning his former love —unborn baby and all.

In *Executive Suite* (1954) she was Paul Douglas's mistress. And in *The Big Knife* (1955) she

was a Hollywood chippy with a big mouth who ran afoul of studio tyrant Rod Steiger and ended up dead.

As mentioned earlier, in *Lolita* (1962) she was hilarious as the mother of the title character. Humbert Humbert (James Mason) married her merely so he could get closer to her daughter, Sue (Lolita) Lyon.

In *The Chapman Report* (1962) Miss Winters was married but couldn't resist Ray Danton. In *The Balcony* (1963) she was a madam. The following year, she was a madam again in *A House Is Not a Home,* whose title meant exactly what it said.

She was putty in Michael Caine's bedroom in *Alfie* (1966) and a western camp follower in a camp western of 1968 called *The Scalphunters.* And in

125

Season of Passion. In the same film, John Mills was Borgnine's pal, paired with another hooker, Angela Lansbury, seen above in the background. (United Artists, 1959)

Mister Buddwing. Angela Lansbury, an actress of considerable range, was a friendly woman who tried to help James Garner in this curious movie. (MGM, 1966)

126

Shelley Winters. As she looked in 1944, the first year she worked in movies. It was four years before she got a decent role, in *A Double Life*.

quickie called *C. C. and Company*. Then she was Anthony Quinn's mistress in RPM, in 1971.

The same year she played Jack Nicholson's pathetic and decidedly unglamorous mistress in *Carnal Knowledge*. Hollywood, with its habit of worshipping any actress who dares to go before the cameras without first being beautified, nominated her for a best-supporting actress Oscar, but she didn't get the award.

Although the hearts of moviegoers usually go out to sinful women of the screen who suffer (it's almost always a man's fault), some happy hookers have also proved successful. One of the more effective portrayers of this latter category has been Shirley MacLaine.

She was a good-natured floozie in *Some Came Running*, with Frank Sinatra (1958). And although *The Apartment* had its dramatic moments (including her attempted suicide) it was mostly funny and both Miss MacLaine, who played Fred MacMurray's disillusioned mistress, and Jack Lemmon were widely praised.

1970, she was Jackie Gleason's mistress in *How Do I Love Thee*.

That Shelley Winters is a more than competent actress is not, irrelevant. She has won two supporting actress Oscars and several more nominations. But she was typed for years as a spectacularly available female. Only the restrictions of middle age seem to have rescued her from regular service in screen bedrooms.

On a smaller scale, Ann-Margret has been similarly classified, although her rather meager acting talents make the fact somewhat less lamentable.

After outgrowing the healthy-American-girl image (*State Fair, Bye, Bye, Birdie, Viva Las Vegas*) she went "serious" in *The Cincinnati Kid* (1965) as Karl Malden's oversexed wife. Hers was the only flawed performance in an otherwise well-acted film.

Next came *The Swinger* (1966), in which she was a fairly obvious sex-pot, which unaccountably gave someone the idea of casting Ann-Margret in the Claire Trevor role in a generally dismal remake of *Stagecoach* (1966). In 1970, she was teamed with football star Joe Namath in a motorbike

How Do I Love Thee. Twenty-six years and numerous films later, Shelley Winters played Jackie Gleason's mistress in this movie. (ABC Pictures, 1970)

127

The Cincinnati Kid. Ann-Margret was married to
Karl Malden (more or less) in this story of gamblers,
but she kept letting it slip her mind. (MGM, 1965)

In 1960, she was *Irma La Douce,* one of the happiest hookers on film, once again teamed with Jack Lemmon. The movie was not a smash hit, but her performance was a delight.

In 1964, in *The Yellow Rolls Royce,* she was gangster George C. Scott's moll-mistress who dallied briefly with Alain Delon before returning to Scott. And in 1966's *Gambit* she was a dummy picked up by Michael Caine in an Oriental saloon to help with his nutty caper scheme.

Sweet Charity (1968) was a big budget musical that flopped at the box office, despite rave reviews for Miss MacLaine as a not-too-virtuous taxi dancer. The same year, in *The Bliss of Mrs. Blossom,* she was a bored wife who stashed a lover in the attic. In *Two Mules for Sister Sara* (1970) she played a tart masquerading as a nun.

But surely the happiest hooker in film history

was Melina Mercouri's zestful portrayal of a waterfront whore in *Never On Sunday* (1960). She quite frankly enjoyed her work and her life and observed only one rule—that referred to in the movie's title.

Nine years later, after several attempts to capture the same *joie de vivre* in a succession of increasingly defective roles, she played a Chicago madam in *Gaily, Gaily* (1969) but this, too, was a failure.

Before closing the bedroom door on this gallery of movie harlots, once again some one-shot portrayals of fallen women demand at least token recognition:

Ona Munson as that understanding scarlet woman of the South, Belle Watling, who knew how to soothe Rhett Butler in *Gone with the Wind* (1939).

Vivien Leigh in *Waterloo Bridge* (1940), who

Sweet Charity. Shirley MacLaine played a "dancehall hostess" in this well-made but unsuccessful musical. (Universal, 1968)

Never on Sunday. Melina Mercouri was a delightfully carefree prostitute in this smash hit made in Greece. (Lopert Pictures, 1960)

Gone with the Wind. Ona Munson's profession was never mentioned in this big movie, but Clark Gable (as Rhett Butler) knew he could find solace at Belle Watling's place. (MGM, 1939)

130

Waterloo Bridge. Love has made Robert Taylor blind to the change in Vivien Leigh. He was away at war, and a girl has to eat somehow. (MGM, 1940)

Citizen Kane. Political rival Ray Collins has just revealed Kane's (Orson Welles) little secret to Mrs. Kane (Ruth Warrick). The compromised mistress is Dorothy Comingore. (RKO, 1941)

A Tree Grows in Brooklyn. Everybody loved Aunt Cissy (Joan Blondell, center) even though they knew about her weakness: men. In the scene are Peggy Ann Garner, Dorothy McGuire, and Ted Donaldson. (20th Century-Fox, 1945)

Born Yesterday. The kookiest and funniest mistress ever in the movies was Billie Dawn, as played by Judy Holliday. With her are Broderick Crawford and William Holden. (Columbia, 1950)

turned to streetwalking when she believed Robert Taylor was dead. He wasn't, but eventually she was.

Dorothy Comingore in *Citizen Kane* (1941), as the publishing tycoon's pathetic mistress, whose life he made hell by insisting she could be an opera singer.

Joan Blondell as Aunt Cissy in *A Tree Grows in Brooklyn* (1945). Despite the censors' white-washing, there wasn't much doubt about what Aunt Cissy's "problem" was: men.

Judy Holliday as Billie Dawn in *Born Yesterday* (1950), the funniest, dumbest mistress ever to smarten up and turn the tables on the bully (Broderick Crawford) who kept her.

Rita Hayworth, sultry as the tropics in the 1953 remake of *Rain*, titled *Miss Sadie Thompson*.

Susan Hayward, a semi-hooker in *Ada*, with Dean Martin, in 1961.

Donna Reed as a likable doxie in *From Here to Eternity* (1954), recovering sufficiently from the pointless death of her lover (Montgomery Clift) to invent a more romantic story about him in the film's wryly amusing final scene.

Ada. Susan Hayward was a lady of questionable virtue in this drama. In bed is Dean Martin. (MGM, 1961)

Miss Sadie Thompson. Rita Hayworth starred in this remake of *Rain*, with Jose Ferrer as the smitten preacher and Aldo Ray, above, as the marine. (Columbia, 1953)

Julie Harris as the flighty Sally Bowles in *I Am A Camera* (1955) and Liza Minnelli playing the same character in the 1972 smash musical version, *Cabaret*.

Jo Van Fleet in *East of Eden* (1955), as Raymond Massey's disgraced wife, living on the outskirts of town, where son James Dean goes to see her.

Elizabeth Taylor as the call girl who falls in love (too late, alas) in *Butterfield 8* (1960).

Shirley Jones as a shameless slut in *Elmer Gantry* (1960), the shortened but effective film of the Sinclair Lewis book.

Martha Hyer as a convincingly flashy strumpet in *The Carpetbaggers* (1964).

Lila Kedrova, so pathetic and disarming as Anthony Quinn's romantic mistress in *Zorba the Greek* (1964).

Simone Signoret in two films: as the helpless married woman who is in love with heel Laurence Harvey in *Room at the Top* (1959); and as the touchingly sad exiled mistress of a dictator in *Ship of Fools* (1965), falling in love with the doomed ship's doctor, Oskar Werner.

133

From Here to Eternity. Donna Reed, above with Frank Sinatra and Montgomery Clift, was an engaging hooker in this fine film from the James Jones novel. (Columbia, 1954)

Sylvia Miles in *Midnight Cowboy* (1969), as a hooker mistaken by John Voight for a wealthy patroness.

Jane Fonda, as Jason Robard's mistress in *Any Wednesday* (1966) and, more impressively, as a hooker who gets involved with a private investigator (Donald Sutherland) in *Klute* (1971).

And then there were the three pathetic females in *The Iceman Cometh* (1973), played by Hildy Brooks, Nancy Juno Dawson, and Evans Evans. One of them kept talking about marrying her boy friend, but somehow never got around to it; the other two didn't mind being described as tarts, but became offended when anyone called them whores.

The same year added two more notable fallen women to the annals of screen sin. *Paper Moon* offered Madelaine Kahn as a forlorn hooker who tried to hook on to sharpie Ryan O'Neal, only to be stymied by young Tatum O'Neal. And *Cinderella Liberty* enhanced the growing reputation of Marsha Mason, seen as a sympathetic chippie aided by sailor James Caan. Both actresses were nominated for Academy Awards but didn't win them.

Thirty-five years have passed from Garbo's *Camille* to Fonda's Bree, in *Klute.* For the most part euphemisms have given way to candor, even shock. But moviegoers can still find room in their hearts for hookers—funny or sad—if the roles are well written and well acted.

I Am a Camera. Julie Harris played Sally Bowles, the loose foreigner in prewar Berlin. (Distributors Corp. of America, 1955)

Cabaret. The excellent musical based on *I Am a Camera* had Liza Minnelli in the Sally Bowles role. At left is Michael York. (ABC, 1972)

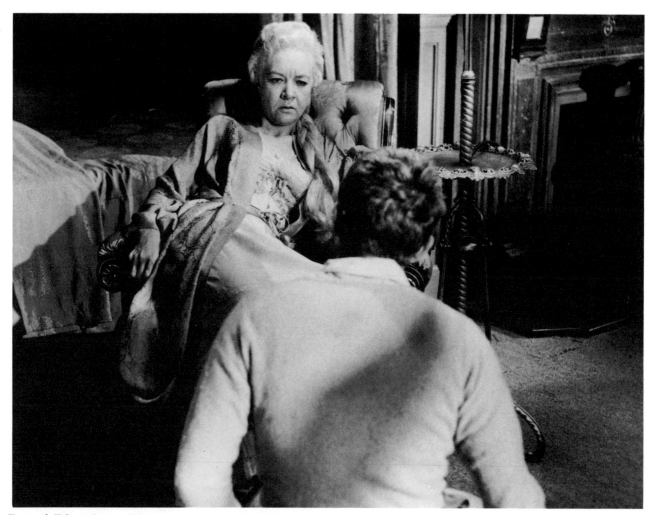

East of Eden. James Dean goes to see his mother, Jo Van Fleet, an outcast with a shady reputation. (Warner Brothers, 1955)

Elmer Gantry. Shirley Jones, right, was the wicked floozie in this version of the Sinclair Lewis book, with Burt Lancaster as Gantry. (United Artists, 1960)

136

Butterfield 8. Call girl Elizabeth Taylor pecks Eddie Fisher, but it was Laurence Harvey she fell for. (MGM, 1960)

The Carpetbaggers. Martha Hyer and Robert Cummings in a scene that pretty well speaks for itself. (Paramount, 1964)

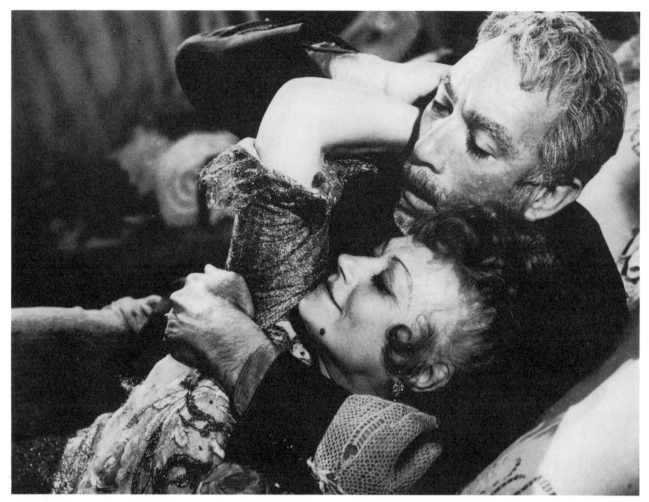

Zorba the Greek. Lila Kedrova was touchingly foolish as Anthony Quinn's sentimental lady friend. (International Classics, 1964)

Ship of Fools. The dying doctor and the exiled mistress fall in love. Oskar Werner and Simone Signoret played the roles. (Columbia, 1965)

Room at the Top. Simone Signoret's fatalistic love for Laurence Harvey won her an Oscar as best actress of the year. (Continental Distributing Inc., 1959)

Any Wednesday. Jane Fonda was usually available for Jason Robards in this comedy. (Warner Brothers, 1966)

Midnight Cowboy. John Voight meets Sylvia Miles, but fails to recognize she's after the same thing he is: money. (United Artists, 1969)

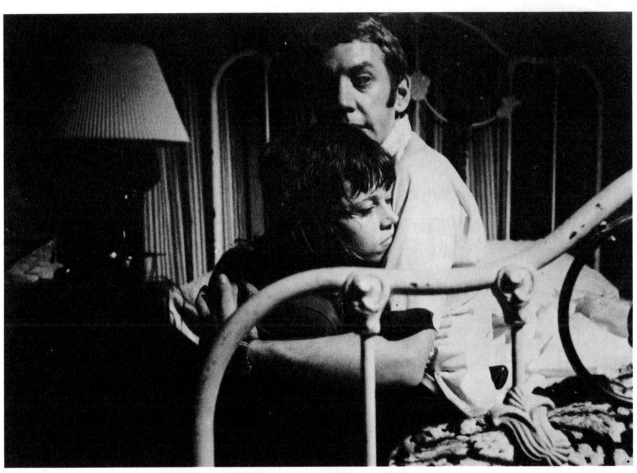

Klute. Jane Fonda was a hung-up hooker in this movie, and Donald Sutherland played an investigator who sought her help. (Warner Brothers, 1971)

6

Sirens and Vamps

The siren, seductress, or vamp in movies is distinguishable from the harlot or hooker in a number of ways.

For one thing, the siren usually wasn't a professional prostitute. Either she was out to milk some dunce of his fortune by marrying him, or she would swindle him out of his hard-earned money and promptly skip town—without ever landing in bed.

For another, she was more often than not played for laughs. Some hookers (Billie Dawn in *Born Yesterday,* or *Irma La Douce*) have been comic characters, it's true. But they were usually likable, sympathetic characters that the audience couldn't resist. The vamp or siren had to be funny straight-faced and expect to be hated by audiences.

Vamps were usually cast for their more obvious physical attributes. (A walk down Mammary Lane could hardly ignore such top-heavy damsels as Diana Dors, Anita Ekberg, Ursula Andress, Jayne Mansfield, Raquel Welch, and Mamie Van Doren.) But it was more than bust measurement that made the successful screen siren.

Finally, it's worth noting that while the hooker is as popular as ever as a screen character, the old-fashioned vamp or siren is virtually extinct—possibly because she was too much of a tease and, not delivering what she seemed to promise, couldn't compete with today's more candid hookers.

Still, the vamp was for long a staple of Holly-wood films and deserves some credit for trying (with rare success) to tempt leading men away from wives or respectable girls next door.

And, as has happened with actresses in other categories, some of the ladies who first gained fame as sirens and vamps went on to become stars of considerable stature—either by playing the same roles in better films, or by graduating to more substantial roles.

Inevitably, Jean Harlow comes to mind. Her career was fairly short but certainly not dull. Platinum blond, a rather nasal voice, not particularly busty, she nevertheless appealed to audiences and in the short space of seven years went from small supporting roles to stardom—and then, quite suddenly, she was dead. She also went from doxie to siren to mock-siren, her screen purity increasing as her star value enlarged.

In *Hell's Angels* (1930) she was a wanton woman. In *The Public Enemy* and *The Secret Six* (both in 1931) she was a moll. But in *Platinum Blonde* (still 1931) she played a society girl who lost out to Loretta Young. In *Red-Headed Woman* (1932) she was a vamp, and in *Red Dust* (also 1932) she was appearing opposite Clark Gable in a saucy but essentially nice role. By 1935, again with Gable in *China Seas,* she was big box office, playing a likable trollop. And in 1936, in *Riffraff,* she stole for Spencer Tracy, escaped from prison, but then promised to go straight.

She was a mock-vamp in *Wife vs. Secretary*

Red Headed Woman. Jean Harlow, the champ vamp of the 1930s, in a scene with Chester Morris. (MGM, 1932)

Wife versus Secretary. Even that wide desk may not protect Clark Gable from the advances of his secretary, Jean Harlow. But note the photo on the desk: Myrna Loy, the wife. (MGM, 1936)

(1936) as the latter half of the title, but wife Myrna Loy managed to hang on to husband Gable.

In *Libeled Lady* (1936) news editor Spencer Tracy uses his girl friend (Harlow) by having her marry William Powell—all this to compromise socialite Myrna Loy and avoid a libel suit.

She died while *Saratoga* was being filmed (1937) and perhaps due to public curiosity it was a box-office smash. Thirty-five years later, the Harlow name still has some of its magic, if only among older movie buffs.

It is impossible to avoid drawing some sort of parallel between Jean Harlow and Marilyn Monroe, if only because they represent—separated though they were by a whole generation—Hollywood's two best comic vamps. Before the first, between the two, or since the latter, anyone else who played a vamp, siren, seductress, or sex symbol was unconsciously being compared to one or the other.

Marilyn's first vamp part was as Louis Calhern's kittenish mistress in *The Asphalt Jungle* (1950). Next came *All About Eve,* in which she clung about George Sanders, the cynical drama critic,

All About Eve. There was too much talent in this Joseph Mankiewicz film for anyone to notice Marilyn Monroe, but she was still noticed. Others above are Gregory Ratoff, Anne Baxter, Gary Merrill, George Sanders, and Celeste Holm. (20th Century-Fox, 1950)

Monkey Business. Marilyn Monroe was an eye-catching secretary in this comedy with Cary Grant. (20th Century-Fox, 1952)

The Seven Year Itch. This comedy really established Marilyn Monroe's image as a comedy vamp. The itchy male is Tom Ewell. (20th Century-Fox, 1955)

barely doing justice to Mankiewicz's lines but looking great. She was straighter but just as sexy in *Clash By Night* (1952), and she was a fetching streetwalker in one of the episodes of *O. Henry's Full House.* As a secretary in *Monkey Business* (1952) she was almost slipping into the Marie Wilson dumb-blond rut.

By 1953, she was a star in *Gentlemen Prefer Blondes,* in a role ideally suited to the Monroe appeal: sexy, vampy but essentially blameless. She did it all over again in *How To Marry a Millionaire,* and better still in *The Seven Year Itch* (1955), as the girl neighbor who is the object of Tom Ewell's itch. The image was further refined in *Bus Stop* (1956) and hilariously perfected by *Some Like It Hot* (1959).

After all the millions of words written since her suicide about Marilyn Monroe—some maudlin, some vicious, some merely foolish—what really matters most is that she, far more than anyone since Harlow, was the ideal comic vamp of American films.

The Blue Angel. Marlene Dietrich was an international sensation in this story of an old fool and a young vamp. The man was Emil Jannings. (Paramount, 1930)

(Some may argue that it's unfair to ignore Mae West, who was in a class by herself as a siren, but it was so manifestly clear that she was kidding all the time that it's virtually impossible to compare her to anyone, or anyone to her. And, perhaps more than any other star in the history of films, she always played herself, with no more variation than was available in her gaudy Gay Nineties Costumes.)

There have been a good many other sirens— some funny, some bordering on the Classic Bitch

Every Day's a Holiday. Some six years after Mae West first slunk across the screen, she made this film, with Edmund Lowe. Wearing enough clothes to cover a chorus of present-day sirens, she nevertheless suggested sexiness. (Paramount, 1938)

Destry Rides Again. Nine years later, Dietrich was as sexy as ever in this serio-comic western with James Stewart. (Universal, 1939)

The Hucksters. Ava Gardner was indeed a tempting dish, but Clark Gable still went home to Deborah Kerr. (MGM, 1947)

or Harlot, some destined for stardom, others doomed to go only as far as their sexy appearance could take them.

There was, to go back to the early 1930s, Marlene Dietrich. From *The Blue Angel* on, she was sexy, provocative, beautiful, seductive. She played harlots as well as vamps, wronged women as well as she-devils. She was never quite Garbo, even less so Jean Harlow. It's interesting to note that by 1939 in *Destry Rides Again,* one of her more successful films, she was already parodying herself. Nineteen years later, in *Witness for the Prosecution* (1958), she was a kind of woman of mystery, sacrificing all for her man (Tyrone Power) only to be betrayed by him.

A "straighter" vamp was Ava Gardner, another beautiful woman who spent much of her movie life tempting men away from more wholesome wo-men. She started, in the mid-1940s, playing molls and the like (*Whistle Stop, The Killers*) and soon graduated to Other Women: with Gable in *The Hucksters* (1947), with Gable again in *Mogambo* (1953). One of her best roles was in *The Barefoot Contessa* (1954), in which she was a tragic woman, gypsy dancer to film star, unhappy marriage, wanton love affairs—the whole works.

That sort of tragic woman role seemed to work best for her: in *Pandora and the Flying Dutchman* and *Showboat* (1951); in *The Snows of Kilimanjaro* (1952); and in *The Sun Also Rises* (1957).

Somehow, she never made it from star to superstar. In 1964, she was a good-hearted innkeeper in *The Night of the Iguana.* In 1972, she did a cameo as Lily Langtry in *The Life and Times of Judge Roy Bean.*

Another effective siren, though never quite a

The Barefoot Contessa. One of Ava Gardner's best roles was in this unusual film with Humphrey Bogart. (United Artists, 1954)

star, was Gloria Grahame, who always managed to look as though she'd been greased to look more sultry. She was fine as Fredric March's faithless wife in *Man on a Tightrope* (1953) and the same year won an Academy Award for *The Bad and the Beautiful,* as Dick Powell's restless wife, running off with Gilbert Roland.

She had been a moll in *Sudden Fear* (1952) and played another one in *The Big Heat* (1953). She was a sex-hungry widow in *Not as a Stranger* (1955) and, for a change of pace, she was in *Oklahoma!* the same year, playing Ado Annie, the gal who just can't say no.

In 1959, she was a neighbor with a yen for Robert Ryan in *Odds Against Tomorrow,* and a western tramp in *Ride Out for Revenge* (1957).

Lauren Bacall, who shot to stardom in the mid-1940s, largely on the basis of a couple of movies with Humphrey Bogart, was an impressive vamp-turned-heroine in those: *To Have and Have Not* (1944) and *The Big Sleep* (1946).

But it wasn't all victories for Bacall. In *Young Man With a Horn* (1950) she was a wealthy seductress who ultimately lost Kirk Douglas to Doris Day. The same year, she was a madam in *Bright Leaf,* but even though Gary Cooper left Patricia Neal, he didn't end up with Bacall, either.

Except for a gold digger role in *How To Marry a Millionaire* (1953) she was through with vamps for a long time—and with films, too. In 1966 she played a rich bitch in *Harper.* After that she turned her attention to the Broadway stage

River Lady. Yvonne De Carlo was in bad company (Dan Duryea) in this melodrama, but, as usual, deep down Yvonne was nice. (Universal, 1947)

again, with considerable success in *Cactus Flower* and even more in *Applause,* the musical version of *All About Eve.*

For a time it looked as if Faye Emerson was going to be a big vamp. She played Other Women in *Juke Girl* (1942) with Ann Sheridan and Ronald Reagan; *The Desert Song* (1943) with Dennis Morgan and Irene Manning; *Blues in the Night* and *Manpower,* both in 1941. Then came *The Mask of Demetrios* and *Danger Signal,* both with Zachary Scott, followed by *Her Kind of Man,* with Dane Clark and Janis Paige, and *Nobody Lives Forever,* with John Garfield and Geraldine Fitzgerald, both in 1946.

In most of her roles, she had some of the iciness of the Classic Bitch, but also the earthy appeal of the Siren. But she drifted out of films in the early 1950s, turning her attention to theater and television.

A sultrier siren was Yvonne De Carlo, who for a time was the B picture Rita Hayworth. When she wasn't trapped in a harem, she was a woman of intrigue, or a saloon singer, or a nice girl with a not-so-nice past that catches up with her.

She was with Tony Martin in *Casbah* (1948), presumably as a follow-up to *Song of Scheherazade* with Brian Donlevy, and *Slave Girl,* with George Brent, both in 1947. Then came *River Lady,* with Dan Duryea (1948) and *The Desert Hawk,* with Richard Greene (1950).

In 1953, she made it into a higher class film

The Big Heat. Gloria Grahame could no more help looking inviting than Glenn Ford could avoid looking interested. (Columbia, 1953)

149

To Have and Have Not. The Lauren Bacall-Humphrey Bogart screen relationship began with this steamy story. (Warner Brothers, 1944)

Young Man with a Horn. Doris Day, sincerely interested in Kirk Douglas's music career, had to pry him away from such distractions as Lauren Bacall. (Warner Brothers, 1950)

Mask of Demetrios. Not all of Faye Emerson's charms could keep Zachary Scott from a life of intrigue. At left is Michael Visaroff. (Warner Brothers, 1944)

Not as a Stranger. Although he was married to Olivia de Havilland, Robert Mitchum was sorely tempted by Gloria Grahame. (United Artists, 1955)

via comedy: she was one of Alec Guinness's wives in *The Captain's Paradise,* and Celia Johnson was the other. And in 1957, she finally made the big time: playing opposite Clark Gable in *Band of Angels*—by now an aging and commercially cooling king, but a king nevertheless.

Another handsomely proportioned miss of the 1940s was Carole Landis, whose frontal appeal helped her stand out in such early small roles as Errol Flynn's secretary in *Four's a Crowd* (1938) and *One Million B. C.,* a prehistoric mishmash of 1940. In *Turnabout,* she and John Hubbard made an acceptable farce out of Thorne Smith's nonsense about a husband and wife switching bodies and clothes. In such 20th Century-Fox musicals as *Moon Over Miami* (1941), *Orchestra Wives* (1942), and *Wintertime* (1943), she was a combination of mock siren and decorative dressing.

She gained some attention in *I Wake Up Screaming* (1942), in which she was Betty Grable's sister, murdered by Laird Cregar, who continued to idolize her. Also, in 1943, she was the busty model helped by fast-talking George Murphy in *The Powers Girl,* but it was her sister (demure Anne Shirley) that he fell in love with.

Her career didn't really go anywhere—some B efforts with Pat O'Brien, Victor Mature, George Murphy, and George Sanders—and then, suddenly, in 1948, she was dead.

There was Arlene Dahl, who did a couple of B

Moon Over Miami. Bette Grable and Robert Cummings did the clinching, and Carole Landis did the vamping. (20th Century-Fox, 1941)

Woman's World. Arlene Dahl and Clifton Webb toy with each other's affections in this scene. (20th Century-Fox, 1954)

films at Warner Brothers before MGM signed her. In *The Bride Goes Wild* (1948), her first at Metro, she was a siren trying to take Van Johnson away from June Allyson. She was leading lady opposite Robert Taylor in *Ambush,* a 1950 western, then prettied up a couple of Red Skelton comedies, *A Southern Yankee* (1948) and *Watch the Birdie* (1950). In *No Questions Asked* (1951) she was a scheming Dahl who ditched husband Barry Sullivan. In 1954, she was Van Heflin's less-than-perfect wife in *Woman's World.* Ten years later, she was a glamorous siren in *Kisses for My President,* which starred Fred MacMurray and Polly Bergen. In between were a handful of potboilers with John Payne, Fernando Lamas, Alan Ladd, and Rock Hudson, none of which did much to improve her stature. Still, in her decade of film activity, she did manage to make some sort of impression as an attractive and sometimes amusing siren.

Early in her career, Miss Dahl was reportedly told by Jack Warner that she could be "another Ann Sheridan." It was one of his less omniscient predictions. Miss Sheridan, who first did numerous small parts under her real name, Clara Lou Sheridan, wasn't really "discovered" until the late 1930s, when Warner Brothers labeled her "The Oomph Girl." She played molls (*San Quentin,* 1937 and *They Made Me a Criminal,* 1939) and somehow conveyed an impression of naughty-but-niceness, which made her an eminently acceptable siren.

Even in leading roles, she managed to walk the fence between heroine and vamp: in *Torrid Zone,* with James Cagney, and *They Drive By Night,* with George Raft (both in 1940).

Her best siren role was in *The Man Who Came to Dinner* (1942), in which she was the glamorous, phony star who pops in late in the film to try gumming up the plot.

But soon the good girl in her image was cover-

The Man Who Came to Dinner. Ann Sheridan, an attractive siren, with Monty Woolley and Jimmy Durante. (Warner Brothers, 1942)

ing up the siren. In *King's Row* (1942) and *Edge of Darkness* (1943) all traces of the Oomph Girl were gone and the "new" Ann Sheridan was somehow a little drearier. She went on for another dozen years, some serious pictures, others mildly amusing, none memorable. A girl who might have become another Jean Harlow was somehow turned into a duller Norma Shearer.

One vamp who succeeded in at least retaining her image was Zsa Zsa Gabor—and it was an image realized in a surprisingly small number of films.

She was absolutely perfect in *Lili* (1953) as a broadly played siren threatening Leslie Caron's romantic dreams until Leslie realized it was Mel Ferrer she loved and not Jean-Pierre Aumont. And though less vital to the story of *Moulin Rouge,* the Jose Ferrer impersonation of Toulouse-Lautrec, Zsa Zsa was ideal window dressing for this Parisian period piece.

In virtually no time at all, Zsa Zsa learned that there was one part she could play better than anyone else: Zsa Zsa Gabor. From then on, she didn't do anything else but, and if this approach didn't exactly make her a superstar, it enabled her to go on for many years to come, doing campy movies, shocking audiences on talk shows, and playing the role of full-time vamp and part-time husband hunter long after many another "glamor girl" had been forgotten.

Lili. Leslie Caron was Lili and Zsa Zsa Gabor was, well, Zsa Zsa Gabor, in this delightful musical. (MGM, 1953)

Moulin Rouge. Zsa Zsa Gabor was little more than attractive window dressing in this story about Toulouse-Lautrec. (United Artists, 1953)

154

Love with the Proper Stranger. Edie Adams and Steve McQueen may look pretty chummy, but the heroine was Natalie Wood. (Paramount, 1963)

Champion. Kirk Douglas was the champion and Marilyn Maxwell was the vamp. But his ever-loving wife was Ruth Roman. (United Artists, 1949)

Getting Gertie's Garter. Billed as Marie "The Body" McDonald, she made good use of her attributes. The man above is Barry Sullivan. (United Artists, 1946)

A few more sirens merit some attention. None of them became top stars, but all of them managed, for a time, to establish a fleeting identity as the kind of girl leading men are sometimes attracted to but rarely marry.

There was Edie Adams, a talented comedienne who spent part of her time spoofing Marilyn Monroe but also turned in some creditable siren-type performances in such films as *The Apartment, Love with the Proper Stranger, Lover Come Back,* and *The Oscar.*

Marilyn Maxwell, a tall and well-stacked lady who should be remembered as a siren tempting Kirk Douglas in *Champion.* She also played comic vamps with such funny types as Abbot and Costello, Red Skelton, and Bob Hope.

Marie McDonald, dubbed "The Body" by some studio genius, tried to make the most of the label in a handful of pictures, most of them underwhelming. One of these was *Getting Gertie's Garter* (1946), in which she played the garterless Gertie.

Marie Windsor had no studio label, but she had some success as a sultry vamp. Her better films included *Force of Evil* (1948) and *The Killing* (1956).

Rita Gam started as part of a gimmick: a no-dialogue movie in 1952 titled *The Thief,* starring Ray Milland. She was also in *Night People* (1954), a cloak-and-dagger story with Gregory Peck.

Going way back to 1940, there was Betty Field, a saucy siren in *Of Mice and Men,* from the John Steinbeck story.

There was Carroll Baker as the provocative thumb-sucker in *Baby Doll,* with Karl Malden.

Rita Hayworth was all siren in the 1957 movie *Pal Joey,* with Frank Sinatra and Kim Novak.

Carolyn Jones was an amusing vamp in *Bachelor Party,* with Don Murray, plus several other movies.

And Sue Lyon proved a delightful siren both in *Lolita* (1962) and *The Night of the Iguana* (1964).

Are some of your favorites missing? Quite possibly. But the line between siren and starlet has sometimes been a fine one, and to cross it would plunge us into a world of Debra Pagets, Terry Moores, and Elaine Stewarts that might better wait for another volume.

Force of Evil. Nobody who looks the way Marie Windsor does here could be the heroine of a movie. The man with her is John Garfield. (MGM, 1949)

Of Mice and Men. Betty Field's aggressive sexiness didn't work with Burgess Meredith, but she sure led Lon Chaney, Jr., into trouble. (United Artists, 1940)

156

Night People. Iron curtain intrigue was the subject of this melodrama. Rita Gam was appropriately intriguing. Also above are Broderick Crawford, Casey Adams, and Gregory Peck. (20th Century-Fox, 1954)

Pal Joey. Rita Hayworth was the wealthy dame interested in Frank Sinatra's career. But he threw her over for Kim Novak. (Columbia, 1957)

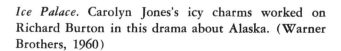

Ice Palace. Carolyn Jones's icy charms worked on Richard Burton in this drama about Alaska. (Warner Brothers, 1960)

Baby Doll. Carroll Baker and Karl Malden in one of the less suggestive moments in this Tennessee Williams yarn. (Warner Brothers, 1956)

Lolita. Nymphet Sue Lyon could do no wrong in the eyes of James Mason, but she certainly tried. (MGM, 1962)

7

Hired Help

There's an old story about a Hollywood school child (in the days when the children of movie stars went to schools in Hollywood) who was instructed to write an essay on poverty.

"Once upon a time," this moppet wrote, "there was a very poor family. The father was poor and the mother was poor. The butler was poor, the maid was poor, the chauffeur was poor, and the gardeners were poor."

If that child was out of touch with reality, what about the rest of us, who watched several decades of movies without ever questioning the logic of Claudette Colberts and Loretta Youngs having maids, nannies, cooks, and social secretaries—along with occasional worries about how to avoid foreclosure on the old family estate?

Still, there it was—escapism, it was called—and we ate it up by the reel without ever worrying about its logic. And a good thing, too, or else a considerable number of actresses might have been out on the unemployment lines with us.

The maid who could rap out one-liners saved many a romantic comedy. The faithful nanny who had some inner reserve of strength has come in handy in many movies. The cold housekeeper, usually belligerent to the new wife, has added chills to some otherwise limp thrillers.

To illustrate how useful Hired Help can be (in movies, that is, and never mind real life) whether serious or comic, let's look at a good example of each.

On the funny side, there was Patsy Kelly. As shown earlier, she played numerous roles that fitted neatly into the Bosom Buddy category. But she was at least as effective when functioning as Hired Help—perhaps more so, for there is an extra appeal to a maid, housekeeper, or cook who can wisecrack with the boss and get away with it. There is, let's face it, a little bit of Walter Mitty in all of us, and it's comforting to see a lowly maid tell off the stuffy Mahster or his snobbish daughter and not only survive but, now and then, prove helpful in solving whatever dilemma the script writers have concocted.

(The commercial validity of this premise was proven anew many years later—if new proof was needed—by the success of the television series called "Hazel," which was based on an already popular comic strip. Miss Shirley Booth, an actress of considerable skill, deigned to play the title role for several lucrative seasons and, to the dismay of her more serious admirers, laughed all the way to the bank.)

But in the 1930s American's image of the irreverent but lovable maid was projected by Patsy Kelly, the Brooklyn pigeon with a disarming accent and a fine sense of comedy timing.

To cite a few examples, Patsy was Fay Wray's maid in *The Countess of Monte Cristo,* in which Miss Wray was a fake countess, thereby making Miss Kelly a fake maid. But a funny one.

In *Private Number* (1936), a romantic come-

Nobody's Baby. Even dressed up to go out, Patsy Kelly could still end up having to do the dishes. At left is Lyda Roberti, Patsy's second partner (Thelma Todd was first) in a series of Hal Roach shorts a few years earlier. (MGM, 1937)

Private Number. Maid Patsy Kelly was willing to help Robert Taylor find Loretta Young, who was really another maid in the same house. (20th Century-Fox, 1936)

dy with Loretta Young and Robert Taylor, she and Loretta were both maids. But, of course, rich Robert didn't know that until the last reel, when love conquered all, including the class difference.

Merrily We Live (1938), another light comedy with Constance Bennett and Brian Aherne, shifted Patsy from maid to cook—but with no loss in irreverence.

And in *The Cowboy and the Lady* (1938) with Gary Cooper and Merle Oberon, she was socialite Merle's maid. The two of them (along with the family cook) went "slumming" one night and met three rodeo cowboys. And the tallest of them was named Gary, who eventually won Merle — while Patsy cornered the laughs.

When nostalgia became America's favorite diversion, early in the 1970s, one of the delights of the Broadway revival of *No, No, Nanette* was seeing Patsy Kelly, older but no less amusing, all decked out in a broad caricature of a maid's uniform. Predictably, she stopped the show at most performances. Not only because she was so funny (which she was) but because the audience recognized one of its favorite Hollywood memories—Patsy Kelly as the funny maid.

At the other end of the emotional spectrum stood a dark, bulky, sweet-faced woman named Louise Beavers. Nobody but a confirmed movie buff remembers the name, but her face is almost as well known as Patsy Kelly's, and her performances as fondly remembered.

Typically, she worked as a personal maid for silent film star Leatrice Joy, later joined a minstrel show, and landed in movies in 1929. Six years and twenty-three films later she was given the role that was to soak millions of handkerchieves across the land.

The picture was *Imitation of Life* (1934) and

Imitation of Life. Louise Beavers's memorable performance in this drama made it all worthwhile. With her above are Ned Sparks and Claudette Colbert. (Universal, 1934)

the stars—in terms of billing, at least—were Claudette Colbert and Warren William. Claudette was a widow with a little daughter, struggling to make ends meet. In comes Louise Beavers, a huge black woman with her own light-complexioned little girl. They team up and later go into business: boxing and selling "Aunt Delilah's" secret pancake flour mix. They prosper and remain close friends and partners, but a tragic cloud looms over Louise Beavers: her light-skinned daughter wants to "pass" as white, rejects her loving mother, runs away, causes no end of grief. In the end the daughter (well played by Fredi Washington) shows up to grieve publicly at her mother's ostentatious funeral.

It was a whopper of a tearjerker and Miss Beaver's fine, subdued playing all but stole the show. True, she was an old-fashioned Negro, content with her lot, respectful of whites—personifying all the qualities that today's blacks reject so forcefully.

But this was 1934, when Negroes really did behave that way to a large extent, and even if Miss Colbert seems mildly condescending in her attitude toward Miss Beavers when you see the film on TV now, that, too, was the way things were in 1934. For all of that, Louise Beavers brought a dignity of her own to the part that more than made up for any obsequiousness demanded by the role.

Alas, although she was in Hollywood films for

Shadow of the Thin Man. **Like most black actresses of the time, Louise Beavers was rarely seen out of a maid's uniform. Here she's with Myrna Loy. (MGM, 1941)**

thirty years, during which she appeared in close to seventy pictures, she was never again to be given a role to equal that one in *Imitation of Life.*

But she kept busy. She played Mae West's maid in *She Done Him Wrong* (1933) and Kim Stanley's in *The Goddess* (1958). And in between she was either cooking for or cleaning up after Paulette Goddard, Carole Lombard, Madeleine Carroll, Lucille Ball, Kathryn Grayson, plus the stars of numerous B pictures.

If she had a dollar for every time she had to say "Yes'm" in a movie, she would have been well off financially. In any case, she died in 1962, remembered still for the moving performance she gave as the warm-hearted pancake maker in *Imitation of Life.*

Perhaps better remembered is another black actress whose career, though a bit shorter, paralleled somewhat that of Louise Beavers. She was Hattie McDaniel, who did manage to do what even Miss Beavers couldn't: she won an Academy Award.

Her face—and possibly her name, too—can bring quicker recognition from moviegoers, principally because she was prominent in one of the most successful films ever made, *Gone with the Wind.* It was as Scarlet O'Hara's gruff but very human "Mammy" that Miss McDaniel won her Oscar as best supporting actress of 1939.

Her scenes with Vivien Leigh had warmth and humor and she projected a kind of stoic acceptance of the way things were (and, presumably, should be) in ante-bellum Georgia. But more moving was the scene, somewhat later in the film, when she tearfully describes Rhett Butler's grief over the death of his beloved daughter, Bonnie Blue.

Hattie McDaniel was not new to movie fans. They had been amused at her pop-eyed, mumbling reactions to the bizarre behavior of the white folks who inhabited the comedies and dramas in which she appeared as maid, cook, or housekeeper.

She was a cook in *Alice Adams* (1935), hired for a "fancy" dinner by Katharine Hepburn's parents, in hopes of making a favorable impression on a new and desirable suitor. In *Showboat* (1936) she was Paul Robeson's wife, confined for the most part to sitting in a rocking chair, shelling peas and tsk-tsking her reactions to anything within earshot.

Even by 1942, a generally admirable film called *The Male Animal,* with Henry Fonda and Olivia De Havilland, gave Hattie the stock role of the

Gone with the Wind. Hattie McDaniel won a best-supporting actress Oscar for her role in this famous movie, playing Vivien Leigh's faithful "Mammy." (MGM, 1939)

funny but likable maid, rather more outspoken than one would expect of Hired Help off the screen, rather less bright than a black playwright might have made her.

Other films in which she was in service include *Saratoga* (1937), with Clark Gable and Jean Harlow; *Nothing Sacred* (1937), with Fredric March and Carole Lombard; *True Confession* (1937), with Carole Lombard and Fred MacMurray; *Made for Each Other* (1939), with Carole Lombard and James Stewart; *The Great Lie* (1941), with Bette Davis and George Brent; and *Since You Went Away* (1944), with Claudette Colbert and Joseph Cotten.

Butterfly McQueen, another black actress whose squeaky voice and baffled manner added some bits of humor to *Gone with the Wind*, also played Hired Help roles in a few other movies: *Affectionately Yours* (1941), with Rita Hayworth and Dennis Morgan; *Mildred Pierce* (1945), with Joan Crawford and Zachary Scott; and *Duel in the Sun* (1947), with Jennifer Jones and Gregory Peck.

If Hollywood filmmakers of the 1930s and 1940s were insensitive to the feelings of blacks of that time, so were most of us in the audience. At least, to counterbalance the Stepin Fetchits, Willie Bests, and other "Uncle Tom" stereotypes of that film era, there was the occasional Louise Beavers, whom no role could demean.

And there have been such other isolated instan-

Saratoga. This time, it was Jean Harlow who had the benefit of Hattie McDaniel's help and comfort. (MGM, 1937)

Gone with the Wind. Butterfly McQueen didn't have as big a role in this one as Hattie McDaniel did, but she still made an impression. That's Vivien Leigh with her. (MGM, 1939)

Cairo. Masquerading as a maid, Ethel Waters was really in this film so that she could join Jeanette Mac-Donald in a duet. (MGM, 1942)

165

Sanctuary. Odetta, known primarily as a singer, did acting chores (plus domestic ones, on screen) in this uneven adaptation of the William Faulkner book. (20th Century-Fox, 1961)

The Man Who Came to Dinner. A startled Nurse Preen (Mary Wickes) is scooped up by Jimmy Durante, as Monty Woolley looks on. (Warner Brothers, 1942)

ces as Ethel Waters in *Member of the Wedding* (1952), Odetta in *Sanctuary* (1961), and Beah Richards in *Guess Who's Coming to Dinner* (1967).

White comic maids, housekeepers, and cooks were plentiful in the 1930s with Patsy Kelly and in the 1940s and later with another readily recognizable actress, Mary Wickes.

One of her best roles was as a nurse. First on Broadway and then in the film version, she was Miss Preen in *The Man Who Came to Dinner*. Gangly, grouchy, and irreverent, she had the thankless task of looking after the impossible Sheridan Whiteside (Monty Woolley) when he broke his leg and was forced to stay in the small-town home where the accident happened. She was a handy target for his jibes: when she knelt down to tuck in a blanket around his legs, Woolley peered down at her suspiciously and demanded: "Where are you going?"

But Miss Preen got her licks in, too. Toward the end of the film, she appeared, bag and baggage, and announced she was quitting. Before leaving, she told Whiteside: "If Florence Nightingale had ever nursed you, she would have married Jack the Ripper instead of founding the Red Cross."

The Broadway performance brought Mary Wickes to Hollywood, where she was to make many a film, and only rarely to escape the category of Hired Help.

But like Patsy Kelly, she had a way of brightening up even the most trivial and trite of movies. One such film was *On Moonlight Bay*, a 1951 musical with Doris Day and Gordon McRae. This was just at the dawn of Miss Day's wide-eyed era and was a routine costume musical in which Doris's parents were played by Leon Ames and Rosemary De Camp.

Mary Wickes was the family cook, now and then offering her unsolicited opinions about the activities of her employer and his family. But she was also provided with a running visual gag that somehow worked: working out of a kitchen with two separate full-length swinging doors, she was

On Moonlight Bay. Mary Wickes made an amusing cook-maid in this lightweight musical with Doris Day and Gordon McRae. (Warner Brothers, 1951)

forever trying to out-guess the restless family members and invariably colliding with one or another of them—always as she was carrying a trayful of dishes.

Save some affection, too, for Connie Gilchrist, a bigger, rounder version of Patsy Kelly. She never succeeded in gaining the public recognition that Miss Kelly did, but Connie Gilchrist's moon face has graced too many films to be unnoticed, and her Brooklyn-Irish speech heard too often to be forgotten so easily.

An outwardly gruff manner characterized her style, but more often than not she was a likable soul in the roles she played, sort of a big-city Jane Darwell.

No doubt, many will recall her as Linda Darnell's hard-boiled and hard-drinking mother in *A Letter to Three Wives*. But that film, made in 1948, marked the halfway point in a career that was to include eighty movies in some thirty years.

She played maids, housekeepers, and cooks in such films as *Junior Miss, Valley of Decision, Good*

Presenting Lily Mars. Connie Gilchrist, as an ex-performer turned charwoman, did a turn with Judy Garland in this warm little musical. (MGM, 1943)

News, Little Women, Auntie Mame, Say One for Me, Fluffy, Two on a Guillotine, and *Tickle Me.*

Now and then, she would escape from the Hired Help category. She was a sneering criminal in *A Woman's Face* (1941) with Joan Crawford; a boozer in *Some Came Running* (1958) with Frank Sinatra; a nurse in combat in *Cry Havoc* (1943); and a nun in *Thunder on the Hill* (1952).

Most memorably, Connie Gilchrist was a charwoman in *Presenting Lily Mars* (1943), one of Judy Garland's less successful musicals, but still a charming one. The movie's best moment came when Miss Gilchrist, bucking up the flagging courage of neophyte Garland, shares the stage in an empty theater with Judy as the two of them sing: "Every little movement, has a meaning all its own. . . ."

Almost in a category by herself is Elsa Lanchester, the wife of Charles Laughton and his valuable aide in a number of his better films. In one of his first films seen in America, *The Private Life of Henry VIII,* Miss Lanchester was a thoroughly enjoyable Anne of Cleves.

Three years later, in *Rembrandt* (1936) Elsa Lanchester was the artist's housemaid who later became his model. Laughton, of course, played the title role. And in 1938, she was a school marm in *The Beachcomber,* once more with Laughton in the title role. They were a great team—he belching and grimacing, glaring daggers at her at-

Good News. That's Connie Gilchrist leaning on the vacuum cleaner, listening to June Allyson. (MGM, 1947)

tempts to tidy him up, she impervious to his jibes, supremely confident that she would bring him around. And for all of Laughton's strong personality, Miss Lanchester always managed somehow to get her share of attention.

She has made a good many films, not all of which belong properly in this Hired Help section. But a few more that do are worth mentioning.

In *The Bishop's Wife* (1947), with Cary Grant as a kind of angel sent down to help clergyman David Niven (the wife was Loretta Young), Elsa Lanchester was a giddy housemaid who couldn't resist flirting with Grant.

Just before that, in 1946, she was in *The Spiral Staircase*, with Dorothy McGuire and George Brent. She was a maid again and she succeeded in expressing the sense of terror that gripped the house in which murder was in the air.

And much later, in 1958, she was back acting with her husband again in *Witness for the Prosecution*. This time Laughton was the distinguished criminal lawyer with a heart condition who couldn't turn down a juicy murder trial. Miss Lanchester was his fussy nurse, nagging him to take his medicine, ordering him about, suffering his insults; but in the end, she took much pride in his victory in the courtroom.

Other imported domestic help, besides Elsa Lanchester, has proved welcome, too. From Ireland came Sara Allgood and Una O'Connor, among others. England gave us Flora Robson and Angela Lansbury.

The Bishop's Wife. The fact that Cary Grant was a kind of ghost didn't stop maid Elsa Lanchester from flirting with him. (RKO, 1947)

169

Gaslight. Suave Charles Boyer took Angela Lansbury's advances in his stride in this chilling melodrama. (MGM, 1944)

ers of butler Herbert Mundin and his wife, maid Una O'Connor. A year later, she was Norma Shearer's faithful maid in *The Barretts of Wimpole Street.* She was a domestic again in *The Adventures of Robin Hood* (1938) and *The Sea Hawk* (1940), both starring Errol Flynn. Eight years later, she was a duenna (governess) in still another Flynn flick, *The Adventures of Don Juan.*

Miss O'Connor's last film, in 1958, was *Witness for the Prosecution* (Laughton, Lanchester, Marlene Dietrich, and Tyrone Power). Once again, she was a maid.

Sara Allgood is best remembered as Mrs. Morgan, mother of the Welsh mining family in *How Green Was My Valley* (1941), and rightly so. But she was sometimes Hired Help, too—a waitress in *This Above All* (1942), with Tyrone Power and Joan Fontaine; a housekeeper in *Keys of the Kingdom* (1944), with Gregory Peck; and a faithful and kind-hearted servant in *Jane Eyre* (1944), with Orson Welles and Joan Fontaine. In 1946, she was a sour-faced nurse working for imperious Ethel Barrymore in *The Spiral Staircase.*

As was mentioned earlier, Angela Lansbury made her film debut in *Gaslight* (1944), as the fetching maid in Charles Boyer's scary London house.

Flora Robson has done a variety of domestic services on the screen. In 1939, she was the housekeeper in *Wuthering Heights,* with Laurence Olivier and Merle Oberon. In 1946 she was Vivien Leigh's faithful maid in *Caesar and Cleopatra* (with Claude Rains as Caesar).

In between, in one of her more mystifying roles, she played Ingrid Bergman's servant in *Saratoga Trunk* (1945). Corked up to look like a mulatto and struggling with a strange accent impossible to identify, she was saddled with lines like: "Your Mama and me promised to take care of you, but it's no use—doit, common doit."

She was far more at home as Susan Shentall's loyal nurse in the 1954 British-made *Romeo and Juliet.*

Thin-faced Una O'Connor fell into the Hired Help category from the beginning of her film career. That was in *Cavalcade* (1933), with Clive Brook and Diana Wynard representing the upper-class employ-

Saratoga Trunk. Flora Robson was Ingrid Bergman's mulatto servant in this one. At right is Jerry Austin. (Warner Brothers, 1945)

The Barretts of Wimpole Street. Sickly Elizabeth Barrett (Norma Shearer) was well looked after by maid Una O'Connor. (MGM, 1934)

In earlier years, kindly looking Jessie Ralph turned up in a number of domestic service roles. In 1934, she was Grace Moore's soft-hearted landlady in *One Night of Love.* The following year, she was Nurse Peggotty in the splendid production of *David Copperfield.* And in 1937, she was Garbo's loving Nanine in *Camille.*

Precisely the opposite in demeanor was Esther Dale, a tall, grim-faced actress who alternated between scowling, disapproving neighbors and no-nonsense housekeepers and cooks. She was a dour and proper cleaning woman in *Crime Without Passion* (1934), with Claude Rains and Margo. She was equally unsmiling as a cook in *Made for Each Other* (1939), with James Stewart and Carole Lombard. She played Bette Davis's straight-faced, straitlaced maid in *Old Acquaintance* (1943).

Jane Eyre. Sara Allgood's ample heart had lots of room for long-suffering Joan Fontaine in this version of the Brontë story. (20th Century-Fox, 1944)

171

Agnes Moorehead, one of America's busiest actresses for three decades, has served as Hired Help now and then. In 1943, she was young Virginia Weidler's pesky governess in *The Youngest Profession*. In 1954, she played Jane Wyman's nurse in *The Magnificent Obsession*. The following year, she was governess to the children of Susan Hayward in *Untamed*. In 1957, she was Kim Novak's acting coach in *Jeanne Eagels*. And in 1964, Miss Moorehead played Bette Davis's decidedly unglamorous maid in *Hush, Hush, Sweet Charlotte*.

That perennial old biddy, Zasu Pitts, in her long career, played a number of hired help roles. In fact, she was a maid (Doris Day's) in her last film, *The Thrill of It All* (1963).

And another actress mentioned earlier in the Bosom Buddy section, Jean Dixon, had one especially enjoyable maid role way back in *My Man Godfrey* (1936). She was the maid in the household where William Powell went to work as a butler and she had something of a crush on him.

Many, many more actresses have done honorable duty in the service of others in Hollywood movies. In their name, let's give honorable mention to one of them: Marie Blake. The name doesn't sound familiar? Perhaps not, but the face is known. She was the switchboard operator at Blair General Hospital in a dozen or so of the Doctor Kildare movies of the late 1930s and 1940s.

Finally, and intentionally saving one of the very

The Lodger. Spooky killer Laird Cregar inspects quarters shown to him by landlady Sara Allgood in this suspense melodrama. (20th Century-Fox, 1944)

Made for Each Other. Esther Dale never served smiles with her food. Also above are Charles Coburn, Carole Lombard, and Donald Briggs. (United Artists, 1939)

Camille. Greta Garbo collapses into the arms of Robert Taylor, as Jessie Ralph looks on. (MGM, 1937)

The Magnificent Obsession. Blinded Jane Wyman had the help of nurse Agnes Moorhead in this romantic drama. (Universal, 1954)

The Thrill of It All. Maid Zasu Pitts lets Doris Day's children (Brian Nash and Kym Karath) stay up to watch Mommy on a TV commercial. (Universal, 1963)

My Man Godfrey. When the socialites weren't around, Jean Dixon could get more attention from William Powell in this classic comedy. (Universal, 1936)

While the Patient Slept. Aline MacMahon, here with Henry O'Neill, turned up in a nurse's outfit in this mystery. (Warner Brothers, 1935)

The People vs. Doctor Kildare. Marie Blake, the hospital switchboard operator, was a fixture in most of the Kildare films. Yes, that's Red Skelton in the center background. (MGM, 1941)

All about Eve. Nobody ever had a funnier maid on the screen than Bette Davis did in this splendid movie. She was Thelma Ritter. (20th Century-Fox, 1950)

best for last, there was the marvelous Thelma Ritter, as hilariously irreverent a maid as anyone ever hired—in or out of movies.

Although she had made a number of films before *All About Eve,* that's the one that made her famous. She was Birdie, personal maid and back-talking companion of Margo Channing (Bette Davis), the Broadway star.

Very early in the film, Miss Ritter set the tone of irreverence to be adhered to thereafter. It was the dressing room scene in which Eve (Anne Baxter) recited her sad (and totally false) tale of woe for Bette Davis and her chums, Celeste Holm and Hugh Marlowe, with Miss Ritter also listening in.

"What a story," Birdie says at the end of the yarn. "Everything but the bloodhounds snappin' at her rear end."

Later, when Eve has wormed her way into everybody's heart (except Birdie's) Miss Davis notices new curtains in her dressing room, made by Eve. Bette is touched, but not Birdie.

"Adorable," she says, with heavy sarcasm. "We now got everything a dressing room needs except a basketball hoop."

(The lines, of course, are the work of Joseph L. Mankiewicz, one of the wittiest and most skilled of Hollywood writer-directors, and there is no intention here to belittle his contribution. But he would undoubtedly be the first to acknowledge that no one could have delivered them better than did Thelma Ritter.)

She didn't always get such good scripts, but she played a lot of servants and aides.

A year before *All About Eve,* she was a maid in *Father Was a Fullback* (1949), with Fred MacMurray and Maureen O'Hara.

In *The Mating Season* (1951) she was a mother-in-law posing as a maid.

The following year, she was Susan Hayward's loyal nurse in *With a Song in My Heart,* based on singer Jane Froman's life.

Rear Window. In this Hitchcock film, James Stewart was confined to a wheel chair and Thelma Ritter was his nurse. In the center is Grace Kelly. (Paramount. 1954)

She was James Stewart's nurse (he was confined to a wheelchair) in *Rear Window* (1954), a first-rate Hitchcock thriller.

In *Daddy Long Legs* (1955) Miss Ritter was Fred Astaire's snippy secretary.

In 1959, she was Doris Day's tippling maid in *Move Over Darling.*

And in *Boeing, Boeing* (1966), she played the somewhat baffled maid in swinger Tony Curtis's lively pad.

During her twenty years in films, Thelma Ritter made some thirty movies and was nominated six times for best supporting actress' Oscars. But she never won.

If good help is hard to get, maybe it's because the pay isn't so great.

8

Witches, Vixens and Horrors

One of the pitfalls of being a glamorous Hollywood star is the fact that sooner or later age vanquishes glamor and anonymity supplants stardom.

Some leading ladies have the talent to manage character parts in their autumn years—and the good sense to age gracefully rather than cling pathetically to what is left of their glamor image. Others are less gifted, less sensible, less fortunate.

The transition demanded by age is usually less traumatic for women who weren't leading ladies to begin with. It is far easier to go from Bosom Buddy to Old Biddy, from Siren to Mother, or from Harlot to Hired Help, than to go from Star to any of these categories. And the work is often steadier, too: one has only to look at the film credits of the Beulah Bondis, Fay Bainters, and Spring Byingtons to realize they have made far more films than the Susan Haywards or Rita Hayworths.

An additional category that has provided work for capable actresses who didn't rely on glamorous images is that of Witches, Vixens, and Horrors.

This class has the extra advantage of attracting attention to the actress in question more strikingly than, say, a maiden aunt or sympathetic nurse. An evil, cunning, totally reprehensible female is more likely to stay in the audience's mind longer than a vapid, bland one.

To start off with a good example, take Gale Son-

dergaard, a respected stage actress before she entered films. She began her screen career with a bang: in her first film, *Anthony Adverse* (1936), she won an Academy Award as the best supporting actress of the year—the first year, incidentally, that award was given.

Although that was a sympathetic role, Miss Sondergaard soon established a reputation as a strong and capable actress in unsympathetic parts. In 1937, she was in *Seventh Heaven,* playing Simone Simon's wicked sister, who whips the poor heroine and drives her into the streets. In *Maid of Salem,* the same year, she was one of the harsh, superstitious women convinced that Claudette Colbert was a witch.

In 1939, Miss Sondergaard turned comedy-menace as a scary housekeeper in *The Cat and the Canary,* with Bob Hope and Paulette Goddard. The next year, she had a good role as the outwardly cool but inwardly seething Eurasian woman wronged by Bette Davis in *The Letter*—and later killing the star.

By now, audiences accepted her as a sinister "type." Consequently, she was in a hokey horror film called *The Black Cat,* with Basil Rathbone and Bela Lugosi, in 1941; and *Enemy Agents Meet Ellery Queen* and *Paris Calling* (both in 1942) in which she had to do her wartime bit—for the other side.

Spider Woman came in 1944, with Miss Sondergaard in the mock-horror title role. And then *The Climax,* in which she was paired with Boris Karloff. And *Spider Woman Strikes Back,* in 1946, the inescapable sequel to *Spider Woman.*

In addition, she was a cold Empress Eugenie (to Claude Rains's Napoleon III) in *Juarez,* in 1939; and in 1937 she had been a sympathetic Madame Dreyfus in *The Life of Emile Zola,* starring Paul Muni.

Her career was cut short early in the 1950s when McCarthyism infected Hollywood. Miss Sondergaard's husband, writer and director Herbert Biberman, was one of the "Unfriendly Ten" who declined to testify before the House Un-American Activities Committee and ended up in prison. Mrs. Biberman has not made a feature film since.

But before the blacklist became a real-life horror,

Gale Sondergaard was a most effective vixen, sneering and snarling her way through good scripts and bad.

Playing unpleasant women, in whatever sort of film, is not a business to be taken lightly, nor one to be attempted by inferior actresses. Besides Miss Sondergaard, the list of Hollywood's most successful female horrors includes such distinguished actresses as Judith Anderson, Flora Robson, and Agnes Moorehead.

Judith Anderson invaded Hollywood in 1940 (along with Alfred Hitchcock) in *Rebecca.* She was the frighteningly demented Mrs. Danvers, the sinister housekeeper so loyal to the first Mrs. de Winter (already dead) that she makes the second one (Joan Fontaine) most unwelcome.

As in the case of Gale Sondergaard, she was im-

The Cat and the Canary. Gale Sondergaard was the sinister welcomer of this frightened group, which includes John Beal and Elizabeth Patterson. (Paramount, 1939)

The Spider Woman Strikes Back. As Rondo Hatton
serves Brenda Joyce, the Spider Woman (Gale Sondergaard) looks fiendishly content. (Universal, 1946)

Juarez. The sight of Bette Davis fainting doesn't seem
to bother Gale Sondergaard too much. She was the
Empress Eugenie, Claude Rains (holding glass) was
Napoleon III, and Miss Davis was Carlotta, wife of
Maximilian. (Warner Brothers, 1939)

mediately typed. The following year, she had the title role in *Lady Scarface,* a ludicrous tale about a woman gang leader.

In 1942, Miss Anderson was with Humphrey Bogart in *All Through the Night,* playing a sinister aide to Nazi agent Conrad Veidt. But she evened the score the following year, playing a fiercely dedicated anti-Nazi in *Edge of Darkness,* with Errol Flynn and Ann Sheridan.

Laura (1944) gave her another good role, as the rich bitch who is keeping Vincent Price. But after the war, she returned to the stage to prove again that she was capable of greater range. Since then her forays into film have been less frequent—but usually in coldly unsympathetic roles.

Flora Robson has twice portrayed Elizabeth I, a queen traditionally portrayed as hard, unlovely, and ruthless. The second time was in *The Sea Hawk,* with Errol Flynn, in 1941. Four years earlier, be-

fore leaving England, she had played Elizabeth in *Fire over England.* It was this unglamorous characterization that led Hollywood to cast her in such trivia as *Poison Pen* (1938), in which she was a bitter spinster who wrote nasty notes. And in 1939, she played Paul Muni's coldly unforgiving wife in *We Are Not Alone,* an unsuccessful version of James Hilton's novel.

Miss Robson's career took her back to England many times, so that the number of her American films was limited. But she kept on playing generally unsympathetic characters for many years. One of her more recent—and least glamorous—portrayals was as China's Dowager Empress in *Fifty Five Days at Peking* (1963) with Charlton Heston.

Agnes Moorehead has already been sprinkled throughout other sections of this survey, but she belongs here, too, having given us several interesting witch-vixen-horror roles.

Rebecca. Judith Anderson scared the wits out of Joan Fontaine, and audiences, as the evil Mrs. Danvers. (United Artists, 1940)

We Are Not Alone. Flora Robson was Paul Muni's cold-hearted horror of a wife in this movie, from a James Hilton book. (Warner Brothers, 1939)

One was as the heavy in *Dark Passage,* a 1947 film with Humphrey Bogart and Lauren Bacall. Bogie escaped from San Quentin (wrongly convicted of killing his wife), underwent plastic surgery to change his face, had a friend get murdered, accidentally killed a petty crook and, finally found out that Agnes Moorehead was the real villain. Then, she very accommodatingly fell out of a window to her death.

Unlike many other actresses, Agnes Moorehead has somehow managed to escape being typed. She could be acceptable in both warm and icy roles. She could be charming, as a worldly French woman in *Mrs. Parkington* (1944) and a society bitch the same year

in *Since You Went Away.* And a year after *Dark Passage,* the Bogart film, she could be James Stewart's loving Mom in *The Stratton Story.*

And she could go from the slovenly servant in *Hush, Hush, Sweet Charlotte* (1965) to a syrupy film like *The Singing Nun* the following year.

It was probably inevitable that when the television series "Bewitched" was cast, Agnes Moorehead got the role of witch Elizabeth Montgomery's funny-spooky mother.

When it comes to versatility, however, some recognition must go also to Elsa Lanchester, another denizen of earlier chapters.

Miss Lanchester it was—the same Miss Lanches-

Hush, Hush, Sweet Charlotte. Agnes Moorehead was only one of the supporting horrors in this gory movie with Bette Davis and Olivia de Havilland. 20th Century-Fox, 1965)

Bell, Book, and Candle. Elsa Lanchester was all witch in this spooky comedy. The laughing man is Jack Lemmon. (Columbia, 1959)

The Bride of Frankenstein. Love finds Boris Karloff. The gorgeous monster he dug was Elsa Lanchester. (Universal, 1935)

Strait Jacket. George Kennedy wants to borrow the axe to kill a rooster. But Joan Crawford had bigger game in mind. (Columbia, 1964)

Johnny Guitar. Mercedes McCambridge was mean from start to finish in this western with Joan Crawford. (Republic, 1954)

The Wizard of Oz. Hollywood's most famous witch was Margaret Hamilton in this fine musical fantasy. The Munchkin at left remains nameless. (MGM, 1939)

ter who had been so effective in genteel pictures like *The Private Life of Henry VIII, David Copperfield,* and *Naughty Marietta*—who leapt to the forefront of Hollywood horrors in 1935 as *The Bride of Frankenstein.* In makeup almost as bizarre as Boris Karloff's, she was truly a fright and a total delight in that highly successful horror film.

More than two decades later, in 1958, she again demonstrated her versatility through two films in one year. She was the nagging nurse to attorney Charles Laughton in *Witness for the Prosecution.* And she was a disarming spook in *Bell, Book, and Candle,* with James Stewart and Kim Novak.

One actress who has been almost consistently evil in her screen portrayals is Mercedes McCambridge. She first attracted attention in *All the King's Men* (1949) as a tough, no-nonsense political henchwoman to Broderick Crawford.

In 1954, she was relentlessly evil in *Johnny Guitar,* a western melodrama that starred Joan Crawford. And in 1956, she was impressive in *Giant,* playing Rock Hudson's bitter sister, jealous of his new bride (Elizabeth Taylor) and afraid of losing her position as mistress of his huge Texas household.

Joan Crawford, incidentally, rates mention in the witch-horror category, particularly with reference to a couple of her later roles.

In *Queen Bee* (1955) she was an unstable type who drove her husband to drink, a friend to suicide, and a former lover to distraction. He finally drove her into a crash that killed them both.

And in *Strait Jacket* (1964) Miss Crawford played a crazed woman who used an axe to chop up her husband and a young lady he was dallying with.

But surely one of the most beloved of Holly-

Margaret Hamilton. Even in civvies she was usually a horror, sometimes harassing harmless types like Percy Kilbride, above.

The Wizard of Oz. The antithesis of Margaret Hamilton was Billie Burke, a sort of traveler's aide for Judy Garland. (MGM, 1939)

Constance Bennett playing an altogether charming ghost in *Topper* (1937), helping Cary Grant make life difficult for Roland Young, but funny for the rest of us.

Ida Lupino, ruthless as the housekeeper in *Ladies in Retirement* (1941), killing her employer in what she regarded as a good cause.

Osa Massen, as Mother Gin Sling (cleaned up from the original stage name of Mother Goddam) in *The Shanghai Gesture* (1942), hardly a distinguished film, but worth remembering for the bizarre characters, of whom she was one.

Gene Tierney, not altogether believable as the selfish wife in *Leave Her to Heaven* (1945), but still giving us a portrait of a coolly interesting vixen.

Ginger Rogers, hard as nails and later revealed as a murderess in *Black Widow* (1954).

Ruth Gordon, totally winning as a gaudy and humorous witch (but no less frightening for this) in *Rosemary's Baby* (1968).

Florence Bates, a nightmare of a potential mother-in-law in *The Secret Life of Walter Mitty.*

And Jessica Walters, an up-to-date horror as

wood witches must be Margaret Hamilton, that bird-beaked little woman who was the Wicked Witch of the West in *The Wizard of Oz* (1939) with Judy Garland. Miss Hamilton made many other movies—usually as a gossipy neighbor or a disapproving old small town biddy—but her superb portrait of Judy's nemesis in that classic musical fantasy etched itself indelibly in the minds of movie fans.

To prove that not all spooks are bad, that same film gave us Billie Burke as Judy's friend, the Good Witch, smiling benignly and helping young Miss Garland to escape the traps of Margaret Hamilton.

Another delightful and harmless witch was the late Margaret Rutherford as Madame Arcati in *Blithe Spirit* (1945), surely a happy medium if ever there was one.

And a few more faces in this gallery of female movie monsters demand a bit of recognition:

A stern-faced Blanche Yurka as the pitiless Madame DeFarge, knitting away as the guillotine chops off aristocratic heads in *A Tale of Two Cities* (1935).

Blithe Spirit. Margaret Rutherford was in touch with the hereafter, with Rex Harrison and Kay Hammond listening. (United Artists, 1945)

she eliminated anyone who stood between her and Clint Eastwood in *Play Misty for Me* (1973).

The last two examples point up an interesting fact. Although movie styles and tastes have changed over the years, and Gale Sondergaard housekeepers or Flora Robson dowagers may seem passe, the recent interest in the occult plus the increasing acceptance of violence on the screen (witness *The Exorcist,* also 1973), make it plain that witches, vixens, and horrors will still be with us in films for some time to come.

A Tale of Two Cities. The center of this ugly group is Blanche Yurka, playing the pitiless Madame DeFarge. (MGM, 1935)

Topper. Those faint images are Cary Grant and Constance Bennett, both ghosts amusingly haunting Roland Young. (MGM, 1937)

Ladies in Retirement. Ida Lupino was the housekeeper who did away with her employer in order to protect her unhinged sisters, Edith Barrett and Elsa Lanchester. (Columbia, 1941)

The Shanghai Gesture. Osa Massen, standing, was a witch of a madam in this potboiler. That's Gene Tierney seated left of Osa, and Victor Mature in the fez. (United Artists, 1942)

Leave Her to Heaven. Gene Tierney committed enough sins in this story that her destination seems unlikely to be the one named in the title. Among her victims were Cornel Wilde and Jeanne Crain. (20th Century-Fox, 1945)

Black Widow. Ginger Rogers, minus dancing shoes, but with enough cold blood to commit a murder in this film. (20th Century-Fox, 1954)

The Secret Life of Walter Mitty. Florence Bates, right, terrified Danny Kaye more than any of his other fantasies. Others above are Gordon Jones, Ann Rutherford, Thurston Hall, and Fay Bainter. (RKO, 1947)

Play Misty for Me. Jessica Walters in one of her calmer moments in this thriller with Clint Eastwood. (Universal, 1973)

9

Bette, The All-around Broad

Anything said in praise of Bette Davis at this late date seems superfluous. Quite deservedly, that great lady has been saluted, toasted, idealized, applauded, honored, and worshipped by fans, critics, biographers, Academies, and late-night talk-show hosts.

That she is the First Lady of film is undisputed. That she has been an actress of compelling force and astonishing range cannot be argued. That she has lived up to the image of a star is obvious. That even now she can command respectful attention by her mere presence is evident.

Why, then, add yet another accolade to the heap of honors already behind her? Simply because she, and she alone, has played—at least once, usually more often—every type of role covered in this survey of Hollywood's Other Women.

It is true, of course, that for a good many years she played only leading roles and thus could not be regarded as an "other" woman in the usual sense. But both before the peak of her screen career and since it, Miss Davis has demonstrated her surpassing talents in a variety of Other Women roles.

Beyond that, there is still another reason. Even when she was the screen's most applauded star, she was set apart from most of her rivals. The Claudette Colberts, Irene Dunnes, and Jean Arthurs stayed pretty close to what was expected of them, what was pretty safe for them.

Of all the leading ladies of the past forty years, a handful might be compared to Bette Davis. Katharine Hepburn certainly has shown equal brilliance. Joan Crawford has demonstrated durability. Rosalind Russell has covered an impressive range of roles.

But Bette Davis has outdone them all. In brilliance, range, and durability, she is unparalleled. Against any other star's top performances, Miss Davis can list *Jezebel, Dark Victory, The Little Foxes, The Letter, All About Eve, The Private Lives of Elizabeth and Essex, Bordertown, Mr. Skeffington, Dangerous, The Petrified Forest* AND *Of Human Bondage.* Plus a few more.

It may simply be a matter of individual taste and preference. No doubt, arguments could be made for Hepburn or Garbo or whomever. But from the viewpoint of this particular survey, Bette Davis is the all-around broad, the champ, the decathlon of dramatic versatility.

To document the argument, it is probably best to survey her roles in the same order in which the chapters of this book are arranged, rather than chronologically. It should be emphasized that this is not a complete listing of all the Bette Davis roles, but only of those that come within the scope of this work.

The strong Bette Davis personality made her eminently acceptable as a Classic Bitch.

In *Bordertown* (1935) she was married to fat,

Bordertown. Paul Muni gives a hand to drunk Eugene Pallette while the latter's wife, Bette Davis, looks on. Later that night she killed Pallette. (Warner Brothers, 1935)

Satan Met a Lady. Bette Davis and Warren William starred in this mangled version of *The Maltese Falcon.* (Warner Brothers, 1936)

jolly, and boring Eugene Pallete. Hungering for Paul Muni, she killed her husband (the old carbon monoxide poison while the car was in the garage bit) and then systematically went after the preferred Muni. When he rejected her (in favor of Margaret Lindsay, it seemed) Bette implicated Muni in the death of her husband. But in a dramatic trial scene, she broke down and confessed. (In 1941, Warners made *They Drive by Night*, a very similar story, with Ida Lupino in the Davis role.)

Miss Davis was a Classic Bitch again in *Satan Met a Lady* (1936), that badly botched version of *The Maltese Falcon*, with Warren William as the private eye. Not too much was admirable about this film, but Miss Davis came through as the cunning, ruthless woman who involves the private eye

in a series of intrigues, all for her own selfish ends. Eventually, she is arrested (as Mary Astor was in the later version) when the private eye declines to play the sap for her.

The film was typical of the kind of thing that caused Miss Davis to rebel against Warner Brothers and try to break her contract. She had already demonstrated far greater ability than was called for in this potboiler, and was to do so many times more. But the studio felt it knew best.

Bette Davis was already a star, however she was treated by her studio. The two films noted so far, contrasted both as to type and quality, show Miss Davis playing Classic Bitch in starring roles.

But she had done Other Woman roles earlier. In *The Rich Are Always with Us* (1932) the stars were Ruth Chatterton and George Brent. Bette Da-

The Rich Are Always with Us. Ruth Chatterton, center, was the star. Bette Davis, left, made a try for George Brent, but she lost. At right are John Miljan and Adrienne Dore. (Warner Brothers, 1932)

Cabin in the Cotton. As indicated by the "lobby card," Richard Barthelmess was the star. He rejected Bette Davis, above, for Dorothy Jordan. (Warner Brothers, 1932)

The Catered Affair. Bette Davis and Ernest Borgnine were the parents of Debbie Reynolds in this comedy-drama. (MGM, 1956)

vis played an interloper, in love with Brent and determined to win him. But in the end Brent returned to Ruth Chatterton.

Although she got top billing in *Housewife* (1934), George Brent and Ann Dvorak were really the leads. Brent played an advertising man who had a spat with his wife, Miss Dvorak. Along came Bette and helped his career, which led him to believe he was in love with her. But he came to his senses in time and returned to Ann.

In an earlier film, *Cabin in the Cotton* (1932), Bette was the spoiled daughter of Berton Churchill (the personification of capitalistic corruption, in those days) and wooed Richard Barthelmess. But in the end he turned to his childhood sweetheart (Dorothy Jordan) and Bette had to be content with a hope that someday he might come back to her.

Miss Davis has played a number of Mother roles, but some of those were leads. We will concern ourselves here, instead, with those roles in which Mother was not the main focal point of the story.

In 1956, fully two decades after she had become established as one of Hollywood's top female stars, Bette Davis was in *The Catered Affair*, a play by Paddy Chayefsky. As the wife of cab driver Ernest Borgnine, she got carried away with unreasonably lavish plans for her daughter's wedding, thereby creating much economic chaos in their modest Bronx home. The role wasn't exactly Bette's dish, but she coped with it in her manner. As one critic noted, she still suggested "a dowager doing a spot of slumming in the Bronx."

Five years later, when Frank Capra decided to remake his successful Damon Runyon story, *Lady for a Day,* he cast Bette Davis as Apple Annie, the Skid Row apple peddler whose Runyonesque friends rally to put on a charade for her visiting daughter (Ann-Margret). Retitled *A Pocketful of Miracles,* the film had a cast that included Glenn Ford, Hope Lange, Peter Falk, Thomas Mitchell, and Edward Everett Horton. Miss Davis had a fine old time, hamming it up sufficiently to be irresistible as the gin-soaked harridan whose maternal instinct is still strong.

In 1959, Miss Davis was opposite Alec Guinness in the film version of Daphne du Maurier's *The Scapegoat.* Guinness had a dual role: an English professor forced to impersonate his double, a Frenchman. Miss Davis was the mother of the Frenchman, duped by his double. Her performance (but not the film generally) was well accepted.

Pocketful of Miracles. Bette Davis as Apple Annie (above with Tom Fadden) was a lovable old boozer in this Damon Runyon tale. (United Artists, 1961)

The Scapegoat. Neither cigar smoking nor playing the mother of Alec Guinness could faze Bette Davis. (MGM, 1959)

Three on a Match. Joan Blondell, center, and Ann Dvorak, right, were the important girls in this early talkie. Bette Davis, at left, was merely a good friend. (Warner Brothers, 1932)

Kid Galahad. Mistress to a gangster, but in love with the bellhop who was turned into a prize fighter. That was the Bette Davis role, and Wayne Morris was the Kid. (Warner Brothers, 1937)

In *The Empty Canvas* (1964) Bette Davis was the estranging mother triumphant. Although it was a pretentious film, Miss Davis was still interesting as the grisly mother of Horst Buchholz, a failure as an artist whose lover-model (Catherine Spaak) abandons him, whereupon Miss Davis helps restore his shattered health.

Bette's finest mother-estranger role came in the same year, in *Where Love Has Gone,* a turgid drama seemingly based on the tragic incident in real life involving Lana Turner, her friend, and her daughter.

Susan Hayward and Joey Heatherton were mother and daughter here, with Bette Davis as the domineering mother of Hayward, largely responsible for wrecking Susan's life and continuing to meddle in everyone else's until she is gratifyingly told off. The role was not designed to create sympathy, and all of Bette Davis's accumulated screen bitchery was skillfully utilized to make this harpy of a mother the most memorable character in the film. Gladys Cooper couldn't have handled it better.

Early in her career, Bette Davis played a couple of Bosom Buddy roles. In a 1931 version of *Waterloo Bridge,* she was the sister of the hero (Kent Douglas, later Douglass Montgomery). He fell in love with a prostitute (Mae Clark). It was Bette's lot to be absolutely delighted over the engagement, never suspecting that her well-bred brother was about to marry beneath his social class.

A year later, Miss Davis was Bosom Buddy to Ann Dvorak and Joan Blondell in *Three on a Match.* Playing a serious young working girl, she had little to do but exude loyalty. As the leading man, Warren William married Ann Dvorak, who later went astray, then hired Bette to look after their infant son. He later fell in love with Joan Blondell.

In *Kid Galahad* (1937) Miss Davis co-starred with Edward G. Robinson, but it was a kind of Other Woman role. Robinson was a fight promoter, she his mistress. Together they discover Wayne Morris, the Kid Galahad of the title, and make him a boxing star. Bette falls for him, but Morris falls for Robinson's kid sister, Jane Bryan. In the end, Robinson is killed by mobsters, Morris embraces Jane, and Bette is left feeling noble.

Over the years, Miss Davis has been an Old Biddy and/or Maiden Aunt a number of times.

The Private Lives of Elizabeth and Essex. Bette Davis made a fiery queen and Errol Flynn was her flamboyant suitor. (Warner Brothers, 1939)

There were, to begin with, her two portrayals of Queen Elizabeth I. In 1939, she starred opposite Errol Flynn in *The Private Lives of Elizabeth and Essex.* Whatever faults the critics found with this Warners version of history, Miss Davis was widely acclaimed for "daring" to appear unglamorous. As Elizabeth, she was aged, her forehead shaved; she was strident, imperious, and she made Elizabeth a fascinating character. Sixteen years later, in 1955, she played Elizabeth again in *The Virgin Queen,* with Richard Todd as Sir Walter Raleigh. Once again she dominated the screen with her shrewd interpretation of a complex sovereign.

In 1945, Miss Davis starred in Emlyn Williams's hit play, *The Corn Is Green,* playing a spinster school teacher whose faith in the brain of a young miner (John Dall) becomes the focal point of her otherwise drab life. No sacrifice was too great for Miss Moffatt to make for the education and welfare of young Morgan Evans; and no actress could have made the character of the teacher so rich and appealing.

Miss Davis was an old biddy again in *Storm*

The Virgin Queen. This time around Richard Todd
impersonated Walter Raleigh, but Bette Davis was
still the queen. (20th Century-Fox, 1955)

Storm Center. A brave protest against book burning
was this little drama, with Bette Davis (above with
Alice Smith) as a small town librarian. (Columbia,
1956)

The Corn Is Green. Bette Davis as Miss Moffatt, school teacher in Wales. Nigel Bruce, above, was skeptical about her plans to start a school for miners, but he melted. (Warner Brothers, 1945)

Of Human Bondage. Mildred, the Somerset Maugham tart, was unforgettably portrayed by Bette Davis in this version of the story, which co-starred Leslie Howard. (RKO, 1934)

Center (1956), this time a small-town librarian caught up in the tide of the McCarthy era. The film was a little preachy (against book burning) but Miss Davis managed to bring some dignity and style to the role of the old librarian who fought for academic freedom.

When it came to harlots and fallen women, few could match Bette Davis in her prime. There was, first of all, her memorable Mildred in *Of Human Bondage* (1934), playing opposite Leslie Howard. She did not win an Academy Award for this performance, but, as has happened on numerous occasions, she got it the following year for *Dangerous,* in which she played a fading actress who turned to drink.

In *Marked Woman* (1937), she was a clip-joint hostess. This was as close as Hollywood dared come in those days to identifying organized prostitution. The Lucky Luciano-type white slaver was Eduardo Cianelli, and Humphrey Bogart was the special prosecutor who sought the help of Bette and the other girls to get Cianelli jailed. The film was a topically oriented melodrama, but it helped cement Bette Davis's already solid reputation as a strong and bold actress.

Somerset Maugham's play *The Letter* (1940) gave Miss Davis another opportunity to play an unfaithful and ruthless woman. Married to Herbert Marshall, she murders her lover (David Newell) and then claims it was self defense. Her cuckolded husband believes her, but in the end the whole story comes out and Bette, acquitted in court, is

Marked Woman. One of a number of girls working for a racketeer was Bette Davis, here being urged by prosecutor Humphrey Bogart to make a clean breast of it. (Warner Brothers, 1937)

the death of Brent (in a duel to defend her honor) and tries to win Fonda back from his new bride, Margaret Lindsay. It was an irresistible performance in a well-made picture. More than that, it seemed the perfect role for the Davis style.

She was something of a Siren, too, in a 1942 film, *In This Our Life.* The spoiled daughter of a neurotic mother (Billie Burke, of all people), Bette is engaged to George Brent, but instead runs off with Dennis Morgan. When Morgan commits suicide, Bette returns to wooing Brent, who is now in love with Bette's sister, Olivia de Havilland. Unable to win him back, she goes berserk, causes a death, and allows a hired hand to be charged with her crime. Finally, she is conveniently dispatched in a car accident.

In the Hired Help category, Miss Davis has given faithful service. In *All This and Heaven, Too* (1940) she was the governess to the children of Duc Charles Boyer and Duchess Barbara O'Neil. The unbalanced duchess resents Bette, suspects her of playing around with the duc. After

The Letter. Bette Davis in another Maugham story. The cold look on her face tells as much as the smoking gun does: she just killed her lover. (Warner Brothers, 1940)

herself killed by the lover's widow, Gale Sondergaard.

An even more colorful role, though not as widely heralded a film, was that of Claude Rains's vain and selfish wife in *Mr. Skeffington* (1944). Having married him partly for his money, she leaves him and takes up with a succession of lovers. When she is old and has lost her beauty, she returns to her now blinded ex-husband, who still loves her and still thinks she is beautiful.

One of Bette's two Academy Awards was in a role that could be regarded as a combination: Classic Bitch, Siren, and Heroine all rolled into one. The film was *Jezebel* (1938) and her co-stars were Henry Fonda and George Brent. As the willful Southern belle who toys with men's affections, she switches allegiance from Fonda to Brent and back again. Along the way she brings about

Mr. Skeffington. Bette Davis was the wife of Claude Rains in this drama, but not a very good wife. (Warner Brothers, 1944)

Jezebel. Scandalized by Bette Davis's revealing dress, the whole town shuns her, but gallant Henry Fonda insists on dancing with her. (Warner Brothers, 1938)

In This Our Life. Bette Davis and Olivia de Havilland were sisters, but Miss Davis was by far the more evil (and interesting) one. (Warner Brothers, 1942)

All This and Heaven Too. Tears streak down her face as Bette Davis testifies in court in this still-popular drama. (Warner Brothers, 1940)

The Man Who Came to Dinner. The man was Monty Woolley, and Bette Davis was his secretary, who longs to get away from her demanding boss. (Warner Brothers, 1941)

a somber series of suicides, deathbed scenes, and the like, Bette returns to America to become a school teacher and be consoled by Jeffrey Lynn.

The following year, she played Monty Woolley's loyal, long-suffering secretary in *The Man Who Came to Dinner.* She finally escapes his tyrannical world and runs off with a small-town newspaperman (Richard Travis). The comedy, based on the Moss Hart-George S. Kaufman play, was one of Bette's few lighter roles, but she handled it with her usual skill.

A quarter of a century later, Miss Davis was working as hired help again in *The Nanny* (1965), in which she was a governess who turned out to be a killer. It was a well-made suspense story, with Miss Davis again striding off with the acting honors.

The Nanny could also fit into the Witches, Vixens, and Horrors category. But Bette Davis has other credentials here, too, which establish her firmly as one of the women audiences enjoyed hating.

One of her strongest roles was as the pitiless Regina in *The Little Foxes* (1941), based on Lillian Hellman's play. All poise and control, she manipulates the fortunes of the greedy family she dominates. When it becomes useful to her ambitions to get rid of her invalid husband (poor old Herbert Marshall again) she coldly lets him die rather than give him the medicine that could save his life. She was magnificently evil.

Twenty years later, at a time when some might have considered Bette Davis finished, she came through with a bizarre performance as a horror in the famous *What Ever Happened to Baby Jane?* (1961). She and Joan Crawford were sisters in this gaudy horror movie. Both were suitably flamboyant, but Bette was the batty one, playing a former child star who still believes she can make a comeback. Before the film ended, she had tortured Joan, killed a servant, and elicited a fair number of screams from the audience.

In the 1960s, as in every other decade of films, the sequel was inescapable when the first film was successful. So Miss Davis was teamed with Olivia de Havilland (presumably Miss Crawford had had enough) for *Hush, Hush, Sweet Charlotte,* another gothic chiller. This time, the madness was spread around: Olivia and Joseph Cotten plotted against Bette; Olivia killed Agnes Moorehead, Bette's faithful servant; and Bette finally did away with Cotten and Olivia. The movie wasn't as unusual as *Baby Jane,* but it still did well and Miss Davis added another portrait to her gallery of ghouls.

The Nanny. Not all of Jill Bennett's cries of agony can move Bette Davis, despite the warmth usually expected of nannies. (20th Century-Fox, 1965)

The Little Foxes. Teresa Wright looks concerned about the illness of her father, Herbert Marshall. But Bette Davis, the mother, can't wait for him to die. (RKO, 1941)

What Ever Happened to Baby Jane? Bette Davis and Joan Crawford were both pretty horrible in this chiller, but Bette was slightly battier. (Warner Brothers, 1961)

Hush, Hush, Sweet Charlotte. This time, Olivia de Havilland was as much a horror as Bette Davis was. And Joseph Cotten and Agnes Moorehead weren't much more lovable. (20th Century-Fox, 1964)

As if the lengthy list of her acting credits in itself doesn't prove her versatility, Miss Davis had yet other ways to do this. In two films she played dual roles, one side contrasted from the other.

In 1946, she double-starred in *A Stolen Life,* playing identical twins, both in love with the same man. One sister was introspective, serious; the other vivacious and forward. When the flashy sister takes Glenn Ford away from the shy one, an unexpected development gives the quiet sister the chance to pose as the other one. (Perky Bette drowns and Drab Bette survives but switches identities.) Eventually, Glenn realizes which sister is alive and, happily, that this is the one he really loved all along.

And in 1964, Bette did a switch on this in *Dead Ringer,* again playing sisters. One sister does away with the other, then poses as the dead

one. It got pretty involved after that, and not terribly convincing, but Bette had a field day playing both sides of the twin role.

Two other combination roles are worthy of mention. One was in *The Old Maid* (1939), in which Bette played an unwed mother who was forced to turn her child over to her own sister (Miriam Hopkins) for upbringing, and then sit by and play maiden aunt for the rest of her life. It was a touching role, a natural for the women in the theater who could weep buckets over Bette's travails.

The other was in the film that many Davis fans regard as her greatest performance. This was the justly famous *All About Eve* (1950), made at what might be termed the peak of her stardom. In fact, the role was not dual. She played Margo Channing, fortyish Broadway star, worried about los-

A Stolen Life. Glenn Ford with one of the two Bette Davises who starred in this love story. (Warner Brothers, 1946)

Dead Ringer. Bette Davis times two. She was twins again, and one sister disposed of the other. (Warner Brothers, 1964)

The Old Maid. The look of longing on Bette Davis's face tells the story: that's really her daughter with Donald Crisp, but she can't tell the world. (Warner Brothers, 1939)

ing her younger lover, plotted against by the ambitious Eve (Anne Baxter), a victim of her own ego and insecurity.

It was a fascinating role in which an actress of Bette Davis's proven skills could explore the various sides of a complicated, three-dimensional character. As realized by Miss Davis, Margo Channing was part heroine, part bitch, part martyr, part harpy. It was a tour de force, and if Bette Davis had never made another film after that she could still have laid claim to the title of Queen of American movies.

It may seem inconsistent to call someone a queen or a first lady and yet include her in a survey of Other Women. But the evidence is ample that her remarkable career has included the whole spectrum of Other Women roles covered in this book, and to ignore her substantial contributions to this gallery of film actresses would be both unjust and ungallant.

She deserves—as do all the ladies in this volume—the respect and admiration of countless millions of movie fans for making women on the screen the fascinating creatures they are in real life.

208

All about Eve. The quintessential Bette Davis, here
with Gary Merrill, in one of her greatest roles. (20th
Century-Fox, 1950)

Index

211